Fabulous Provinces

Three generations of the Young family; the author is in second row, extreme left

University Press of Mississippi
Jackson

Fabulous Provinces
A Memoir

Thomas Daniel Young

Copyright © 1988 by the *University Press of Mississippi*
All rights reserved
Manufactured in the United States of America

This book has been sponsored
by the *University of Southern Mississippi*

Library of Congress Cataloging-in-Publication Data

Young, Thomas Daniel, 1919–
   Fabulous provinces : a memoir / Thomas Daniel Young.
    p. cm.
   ISBN 0-87805-350-6
   I. Title.
PS3575.O854F3 1988
813'.54--dc19   87-35340
                                                                                   CIP

British Library Cataloguing-in-Publication data is available.

CONTENTS

    Preface   vii
1 Son, Are You a Doctor?   3
2 Doctor Young Coleman   10
3 Think You Can Handle the Fourth Grade?   18
4 Lula, that New Car of Yours Has Bad Habits   34
5 Listen to Leon   45
6 What Do You Plan to Do?   54
7 Look at this Program   65
8 This Might Be Your Only Chance to Meet Faulkner   75
9 A Kind of Doctor that Can't Do Anyone Any Good   93
10 I Hear You Got Hired   105
11 Do Not Go Beyond this Point Unless You Know the Way Is Clear   116
12 Reading Good Books   128

For
Janey, Myrta, and Mary
 and
In memory of Edwin and Madge

Philomela, Philomela, lover of song,
I am in despair if we make us worthy,
A bantering breed sophistical and swarthy;
Unto more beautiful, persistently more young,
Thy fabulous provinces belong.

From "Philomela"

John Crowe Ransom
Selected Poems

PREFACE

In the spring of 1958, just before leaving Delta State College, I received a letter from my mother. There was to be a program commemorating my father for his fifty years of service to the citizens of the Bond community, and she had been asked by Grady Barnhill, an employee of the post office in a nearby town, to invite me to say a few words of response, representing the family's appreciation of this honor which the community was conferring on my father. Of course, I accepted, and for the next few days my mind was occupied with what I should say, attempting to represent my father who was physically unable to respond for himself.

On the evening of October 4, 1958, the auditorium of Bond High School was filled. Those who could not find seats stood at the back of the auditorium, and some who could not get inside were standing on the porch outside. Some of those seated on the platform had done considerable research. When called on, one arose and reported how many babies my father had delivered (just over 4,000). After he had read the information he had received from the Bureau of Vital Statistics in Jackson, the speaker asked if all those in the audience who were "Doc's babies" would stand (all of them had been pinned with blue ribbons), and it seemed that half of those present did so. The speakers gave examples of my father's skill and devotion. One person told how "Doc stayed with grandmother for three weeks solid while she was getting over being bitten by a snake when she was picking blackberries." Another told of my father's sleeping "at our house for three weeks when Mama had pneumonia." The other accounts followed this pattern.

Grady Barnhill was the master of ceremonies. In his remarks, Grady casually mentioned that he "was Doc's first patient." This remark piqued my interest. When I asked about it later, I was told the story presented in this book. In doing so, I have added only direct conversations that were reported to me indirectly. All the characters are based on real persons. For the sake of unity, only occasional liberties with the facts were taken. What I have attempted here is to present representative events, episodes, and persons that accurately portray social, economic, and cultural developments during the first seven decades of this century. To be more specific, I have tried to present—from the point of view of a first-person narrator, not always the author—what it was like to grow up in Mississippi between 1900 and 1950. I hope, as well, that I have pointed up the difference between the sociological term *plane of living* and the expression popular among humanists, *quality of life*, and by doing so suggest why the South, the region with the country's lowest standard of living, was at same time its literary center.

Fabulous Provinces

CHAPTER

1

Son, Are You a Doctor?

Will was almost asleep when the conductor suddenly opened the door of the day coach and yelled, "Artesia, next stop! Artesia in five minutes." He sat up, stretched, and stepped into the aisle and began collecting his luggage. He pulled down an old cardboard valise that contained almost all of his worldly belongings, then, more carefully, laid beside it a paper bag in which were packed scissors, forceps, bandages, stethoscope, and assorted salves and pills. He had been given these items the evening before, following his graduation from the University of Nashville School of Medicine. At the reception honoring the graduates, each brand-new M.D. had been given the same packet. Will had just written his name on the package and was going to leave it in the library when he encountered Dr. Larkin Smith. Smith, his favorite teacher, examined the contents of the parcel. "They've given you everything you will need to practice medicine," Dr. Smith remarked (sarcastically, Will thought), since it had been Smith who had consistently—and alone among Will's teachers—emphasized that disease is caused by bacteria. It was true that others had *mentioned* the possibility as an interesting theory, but these men remained committed to the notion that some maladies were caused "by breathing the unwholesome damps" while others were caused by an excess of the "humors"·

and could be treated successfully by removing the contaminated blood. In exasperation Dr. Smith had once remarked to his class: "The only skills we have taught you are how to set a broken bone and how to assist in the birth of a child. In addition, you have been instructed in the proper manner of administering quinine and calomel."

As soon as he could do so without committing a breach of etiquette, Will slipped away from the reception and hurried to his boarding house to get his bag, already packed. He had little time to spare if he was going to catch the late-night, south-bound train. He wanted to visit his family before looking for a place to set up practice. Will arrived at Nashville's Union Station, then recently opened, and purchased a ticket for Meridian, Mississippi. He got himself settled in a double seat so he would have room to stretch out and get some sleep. Once he reached Meridian, he still had a full day's ride on horseback before he reached the family home in Neshoba County, between De Kalb and Philadelpha.

Shortly after daylight, he reached Artesia. It would be three hours before a train came through that would take him to Meridian. He got off the train and walked along the platform, looking for a quiet spot in which to take a nap while he waited for his train. As he was trying to decide between a seat in the small, dilapidated station and one under a big oak tree, he heard a voice yelling, "Warm chicken. Good cornbread." He turned. Approaching was a large woman with a white apron and matching scarf on her head. She was pulling a home-made wagon. Realizing that he hadn't eaten since the previous evening, he waited. When the woman—who looked like the stereotypical Southern black cook—got within hearing range, he asked how much there was in the bags she was selling. "A bellyful, white boy," she replied. Will bought a bag and, having decided on the oak tree, sat down to a feast of chicken wing, thigh, breast, and two generous squares of cornbread.

As Will sat eating his breakfast, he noticed a livery stable across the way. It looked like it held ten or twelve horses. As he sat there, a new plan gradually took shape in his mind: Why not cash in the unused portion of his ticket, buy one of those horses, and ride it home? The journey would be only slightly longer than the one he now faced from Meridian; and besides, he could be on the lookout as he rode for a possible place to set up practice.

By the time Will had finished eating, his mind was made up. He went across to the livery stable and asked about the price of a horse. After some haggling, he found that for forty dollars he could buy a sturdy-looking roan with a white blaze down her face and a saddle with large saddle bags. By cashing in the unused portion of his ticket and using the cash he had left, Will found that he had money to buy the horse and enough food for himself and it to get them to their destination. He might even find a suitable place to set up practice enroute. Besides, he had been cooped up in a city for too long.

Will bought the horse and saddle, emptied his medical instruments and supplies into the saddle bags, and got an empty feed sack from the owner of the livery stable. He fastened the saddle bags, put his clothes in the feed sack, mounted the horse, and rode off toward Macon, happier than he had been since leaving home more than four years earlier.

As he made his way to Macon and then west toward Louisville, he noticed the change in terrain through which he was traveling. The black, level prairie gradually merged into rolling hills covered with virgin pine timber. The land was similar to that of his native Neshoba County. Occasionally he saw a small homestead made by cutting the pines, dragging them into piles, and burning them. At other times he saw evidence that logging crews had passed through large areas, cutting the trees they needed to supply the sawmills that were becoming more plentiful in the area. Mill owners seeking the best trees made no attempt to preserve those unsuitable or less suitable for their purposes. This heedless destruction of the region's principal source of wealth came about because there seemed to be an inexhaustible supply of three-foot pines rising almost limbless for a hundred feet.

As darkness closed in, Will grew afraid that his horse might step in a hole and break a leg; so he decided to stop until daylight. He fed and tethered the mare, then set about preparing supper. He ate part of the piece of cheese he had bought in Artesia and half a can of Vienna sausage. After checking his horse to make sure she was still securely fastened, he set about making himself as comfortable as possible for the night, rolling himself in the blanket he had taken from his sack of clothes and laying his head on the saddle. As he lay there listening to the mosquitoes buzzing around his head, he wondered whether he had made the right decision in abandoning the train and setting out on horseback. He thought about the classmate who had invited Will to join him in forming a partnership in Meridian but for the thousandth time reassured himself that that was not the kind of practice *he* wanted. He was a country boy; he didn't want to be office-bound. He much preferred to move about the country seeing his patients. Of course, he wanted access to a hospital, so that patients too ill to be treated at home or in his office could be given proper care. Will also wanted to own some land and to have the opportunity to engage in businesses other than medicine. With these ideas occupying his thoughts, he soon was overcome by the need for sleep and gradually surrendered to the need. Until the sun from a cloudless sky shone directly in his eyes, he was oblivious to the world.

He and the horse quickly ate and they set off. Nearly six hours later, they approached a hamlet which consisted of a dozen dwellings clustered loosely around a large steam-powered sawmill and a rambling, unpainted general store, which included a post office. A blacksmith shop was next door. Since he was in completely unfamiliar territory, Will, after letting the horse drink from a trough beside the store, decided he had better get some food for himself and the horse. He had no idea when he would find another store. He tied the horse to a hitching post and walked through the front door. As his eyes gradually adjusted to the gloomy interior, he was struck by the aroma of leather, cheese, apples, and aging wood—altogether, a pleasant aroma. Then a voice asked from the back of the store, "Can I do something for you?" The voice came from a wiry little man standing in the enclosure at the back of the store marked POST OFFICE, BOONE, MISSISSIPPI.

"Yes. I need some dinner, and so does my horse."

The man closed the latticed wooden gate to the post office and came to the front of the store. "I'm Melvin Barnhill. Don't believe I've seen you before."

"No, I guess you haven't. I'm a stranger in these parts. Just passing through on my way to the Cleveland community, down in Neshoba."

They shook hands and began talking about the weather and the crops; but Melvin Barnhill did not offer to wait on Will. Instead, he said: "I was about to close up here and go to the house for dinner. Why don't you put your horse in the barn and come with me?" Will thanked him, admitting that, since it had been almost two days since he had had one, he would indeed like a hot meal. Barnhill went back to the post office and put up the few remaining pieces of mail, then came back to the front of the store, and they walked over to Barnhill's house together. As they neared the house, about twenty-five yards from the store, Barnhill yelled, "Edgar! Come here!" He told the fourteen-year-old boy who appeared to take Will's horse to the barn, unsaddle it, and give it some corn. Then they went up the steps to the front porch of an enclosed dog-run house and entered a long hall, which served as a dining room-sitting room. Soon joined by Edgar, they sat down at the table. Mrs. Barnhill, a large woman with a noticeable limp, entered and sat at the end of the table nearer the kitchen, where she could more easily replenish the dishes of food on the over-burdened table. Opposite her was her husband and on his right were Will and Edgar. Opposite them were two other boys—Grady, about two years younger than Edgar—and Roy, two years Grady's junior. Before them stood a veritable feast of summer vegetables: new peas and potatoes in a rich butter-cream sauce, fried squash, turnip greens, radishes, spring onions, crusty biscuits, cornbread muffins, coconut cake, and freshly baked egg custard. Beside each plate was a half-pint goblet of milk, which, since it was taken from the cows earlier that day, had cooled in a tightly closed molasses pail at the bottom of the well.

Almost an hour later, Will, filled to capacity, joined the family on the front porch. Melvin Barnhill sat in a cane-backed chair tilted against the wall, fighting food-induced drowsiness. In the kitchen, his wife was clearing the table. The boys were sprawled on the porch. Eventually Grady restlessly got up and went to the front steps. Noticing that he had a decided limp, Will said to him: "Come over here a minute, son. Why are you limping so? What's wrong with that foot?"

"I don't know. Had it a long time. People say I got a bone felon." He sat down at Will's feet, and Will took the foot in both hands. Looking at it carefully, he could see that constant walking in dew-covered grass, farmlots, fields, and woods had not only bruised the foot more or less permanently but had also dangerously infected it.

Will asked Edgar to go to the barn and fetch his saddle bags. When the boy returned, Will removed a scalpel and a bottle each of alcohol and iodine. He had Roy and Edgar hold Grady while he washed the affected part of the foot with alcohol, then lanced it and allowed it to drain. Finally, he applied iodine and dressed the foot with a bandage.

Melvin Barnhill, who had been watching this procedure and great interest, waited until Will had finished, then asked: "Son, are you a doctor?"

"I guess so. At least, that's what they told me in Nashville." Will looked back at Grady. "But let's wait and see if this fellow lives. Then we'll know for sure."

The boy's father considered this bit of wit for a moment. "We sure do need a doctor around here," he said at last, as much to himself as to Will. At the same time, the statement sounded like a question. Melvin was obviously getting at something. "The nearest one is ten miles away, and he's overworked as it is," Melvin continued. "If you'd settle here, you could use the side room where I store feed, and I wouldn't charge you a penny rent."

Will inspected the room and decided that it would do. By early afternoon the next day, they had cleared out the room, and Will hung a sign outside the front door that read: W. A. YOUNG, M.D. Around five o'clock, Will received his first patient, an elderly black man with the "spring mizries." Will gave him a "bedtime capsule" with instructions to take two tablespoons of castor oil before breakfast. The man gave Doctor Young two dollars. Thus began a practice that would last nearly sixty years.

CHAPTER

2

Doctor Young Coleman

Mrs. Barnhill said she thought Mrs. John McGahey, wife of the owner of the mill, who lived across the road about two hundred yards away, would board Will until he could make more permanent arrangements. She sent Edgar to inquire, and he returned a few minutes later, saying, "Miss Ida said she would be glad to have Doctor Young." ("She said she would be glad to help," my father told me years later, "'cause they needed a doctor real bad.") Will closed his new office for the day, then collected his belongings and led his horse down the road until he came to a large white house with a porch across the front and along one side. The latter porch was screened and contained three or four double beds. Apparently the family slept there on hot summer nights. It was one of the largest houses he had ever seen.

As Will approached, the front door was opened by a black boy of about twelve who said: "Miss Ida say I'ze to show ya whur ta put yo hoss." At the barn they were met by another Negro, this one about eighteen. They were both, Will later learned, children of the cook. The older boy took the horse, removed the saddle and hung it in the barn. He led the mare to a water trough outside, then brought her back and rubbed her down. Next, he put her in a stable, where a troughfull of shelled corn awaited. Long accustomed to doing his chores for himself, Will could hardly remember when he had been treated so well. He was just as pleased with the appearance of his room. It was large, at least twenty-four feet square, with double windows on the north and east sides. The furnishings, while not lavish, were comfortable. A large four-poster bed with a deep feather mattress and two double pillows, a washstand with porcelain pitcher and wash pan and two starched linen towels, a rocking chair with an Aladdin lamp on a stand beside it, a desk with a chair and another lamp. All this—capped by a dark blue, woolen rug on the floor and white ruffled curtains at the windows—reminded him of Huck Finn and his impression of the room in the Grangerford home. Could he afford this? he wondered. After a night on the train, followed by one on the hard ground, he couldn't resist it and pulled off his shoes and stretched out. The next thing he knew the young Negro, whose name he learned was Stanley, was calling him to supper.

Supper differed little from the meal he had at noon. There were the same four or five vegetables, their flavor unaffected by being warmed over. In special recognition of their "honored guest," Nellie Ann, the cook, had made a blackberry pie from some fruit she had canned the previous summer and had fried some home-cured ham. Will saw immediately that he could not hold his weight at 185 if he ate two meals this size every day.

They were sitting on the porch after supper, when John McGahey, a tall, slim man of thirty-five, turned to Will and said, "Will, I've got forty families working for me at the mill, and half of them don't get decent care. If you'll see after them, I'll give you twenty dollars a family per year. You can see them at home or in your office. If they have to go to a hospital or if they need medicine, that's extra, and they'll have to pay for that themselves."

Will was nonplussed—again. Here he was, being guaranteed eight hundred dollars a year from a completely unexpected source. All he could do was stammer out, "Yeah. Sure. Thank you very much."

"Good," McGahey said; "I'll have my foreman give you a list of the names tomorrow. Well, it's nearly nine. My bedtime. Ida, are you coming?"

The next morning after breakfast, John McGahey gave Will $200, payment for a three-month period of the contract they had agreed upon the night before. Will went over to his office and there found a young woman waiting with her young son. The boy had dislocated his shoulder. Will felt along the line of the shoulder blade until he found the spot he was looking for. As the mother held the child, he grasped the arm tightly, pulling the dislocated joint firmly apart and allowing it to slip back into its proper position in the socket. Although the child screamed, the mother held him, and by the time Will returned with a stick of candy from the store, he was snuffling and smiling. "My husband will pay you this fall when he sells his cotton," she said as she caressed the boy's face. "Thank you, doctor."

At that point, Melvin Barnhill stuck his head in the door and inquired with a straight face: "How many you killed this morning? I heard one go a short while back." Will assured him he might have maimed a few and some might die later, but so far he didn't think he had killed anyone. After seeing a young man from the sawmill who had crushed a finger under a log he was attempting to get on the saw carriage, Will was idle for about an hour. Since things were slow at the moment, he decided to go into Louisville and buy some furniture for his office. He borrowed a rig from Barnhill and drove into town, which at that time had fewer than a thousand inhabitants. He noticed a building on the southwest side of the second block with a large sign in the window: J. D. MCGRAW GENERAL MERCHANDISE.

Will had a hunch that was just the place he was looking for. He parked in front and went in. A large, portly man of medium height came from the back of the store and asked, "Can I help ya?" Will told him what he needed and soon had acquired a small table, an Aladdin lamp, a wicker settee and two matching chairs, and a larger table on which he could examine patients. He even got a large screen to separate the patient he was treating from those waiting. Will was so pleased that he had furnished his office for so little that he decided to buy himself another suit, to which he added a shirt, tie, and pair of shoes. He needed at least one change of clothes. All he had at the moment was the suit he had bought for graduation.

Somehow he and the merchant found space in the buckboard and on the seat. Then he asked directions to Doctor Richardson's office. Doctor Richardson had graduated from the University of Nashville a year ahead of Will and was now practicing medicine in Louisville. Will still had almost a hundred dollars and wanted to find out where he could get some medical supplies he still needed.

He found "Richy" in a two-room suite above a drugstore in the next block. After expressing his surprise and delight at learning that Will had set up practice so near him, Richy said: "You can get pretty much what you need downstairs, but you'll save yourself money if you order direct from Standard Drug in Meridian. I'll have their salesman stop by to see you next week when he comes through." Then the two schoolmates went downstairs and had a sarsaparilla, and Richy introduced Will to the druggist, from whom he purchased what he would need until he could place an order with the Standard Drug Company.

Will started home in the loaded buckboard well aware that the return trip would take longer than the one coming. Still, for the first time since leaving Nashville, he felt that he was putting down roots, that he was going to be Doctor Young of Boone for some time (though he had no way of knowing that "some time" would be fifty-six years).

By the time he reached Boone and, with help from Grady and Edgar (Grady's foot had improved considerably), it was almost dark. Leaving Edgar to take care of the horses, and after reading a note from Melvin Barnhill telling him that three patients had been to see him while he was away, Will crossed the road to the McGaheys'. There he found a heaping plate which Miss Ida had left in the warming closet. He ate quickly, then asked Miss Ida for some paper and an envelope. It had just occurred to him that his parents would be wondering why he still wasn't home.

The next morning Will went to his office and arranged his new furniture. He discovered that the screen he had bought in Louisville would give precious little privacy for his patients. As he opened the door, he saw a Negro boy standing by the hitching post. When Will spoke to the boy, he handed Will a virtually illegible note on rough paper: "Come quick as ya kin baby comin Levi Coleman." Quickly Will went into the store and asked Melvin Barnhill where Levi Coleman lived. "Go down Skillet Road," Melvin said. "Turn right at the first road ya come to. Stop at the first house and ask." Back in his office, Will gathered up what he would need and set off. He went down the Skillet Road, past the McGaheys' about a mile. When he came to a corduroy road, he turned right. He soon reached the "house" Melvin had referred to (actually, it was a log cabin), where he asked directions to Levi Coleman's. The youngster he asked did not utter a sound but turned abruptly and went running toward the house. "Mama!" he yelled; "somebody wants to go to Mr. Levi's." The boy's mother came to the door. "Is you the new doctuh? I thot it wuz about Miz Coleman's time." Will nodded, and she said: "Go up dat road erbout a quata. His'n is the fust hous ya come ta." Will thanked her and rode until he came to a dogtrot. On the porch of the house, he saw a mirror above a small washstand on which there was a bucket made of rough oak and a gourd. Beneath the mirror was a small shelf that held a bar of homemade lye soap, a mug, and a straight razor. At Will's second yell a young black man dressed in freshly washed overalls and a blue, homemade cotton shirt hurried out of the back room. "I'm sho glad to see ya," he said. "Last time we couldn't git a doctor, and she had a bad time." The midwife had made his wife as comfortable as she could. She sat beside the bed and held a wet cloth to the woman's head. Will examined her, seeing immediately that there was nothing he could do but wait.

Will had assisted with childbirth many times while in medical school, and he knew all he could do was try to ease her pain until the baby was ready to emerge. He went out on the front porch and fought mosquitoes for awhile. When he heard the young woman groan, he knew she was near delivery. He assisted as much as he could, and soon there it came—a boy. He handed the baby to the midwife and went back out on the porch.

"I ain't got no money," Levi said from his chair beside the wall, "but I shore thank you. I got some good shoats that will be ready to kill this fall. I'll bring you two of 'em. The next one, iffen it's a boy," he added as though he had just thought of it, "I'm goin' to name him after you." Two years later the Colemans were expecting another child, and Will and his young bride speculated on what the baby would be named if it were a boy. Would they call it William or Allen, Will's middle name? Or William Allen? When the child arrived, Levi proudly announced: "Dare he is! Named for you— Doctor Young Coleman."

Years later, when I visited the town, I saw a sign on a storefront: D. Y. COLEMAN CONSTRUCTION COMPANY—NO JOB TOO LARGE OR TOO SMALL. Thus, when I read Faulkner, I was prepared for Colonel Sartoris Snopes and Wall Street Panic Snopes. Their names seemed quite natural. But I did wonder what Doctor Young Coleman's friends called him on an everyday basis. Doctor? Doc? Or just by the initials on the sign?

The following Sunday, Will went to church. He paid less attention to the sermon than to the trim, straight-backed young woman who played the organ. At dinner following the service, he asked Mrs. McGahey about her and was told that she was Lula Wright, sister of the local schoolmaster. She was engaged to Doctor Haggard, who practiced medicine in a nearby community. This last information upset Will's strategy, since he intended to ask his landlady to introduce him to Lula. Seeing that such a request was now inappropriate, he excused himself and went across the road to his office, intending to tidy it up and see if he couldn't do something about that inadequate screen in his examining room. He had only a quiet, lonesome afternoon to look forward to.

About thirty minutes later, he heard someone shouting, "Doctor! Doctor!" and looked out the window. There he saw a young black man sitting on a rawboned mule that had obviously been ridden too far, too fast. Will opened the door, and the man—still mounted—said: "Mr. Byron Jernigan is bad off. Miss Ella wants ya to come quick."

Hurriedly, Will went to the barn and hitched his horse to the buggy (still borrowed). The black man tied the mule to the back of the buggy, using a combination plow line-bridle, and got in beside Will. They rode about eight miles, turned up a logging road that led into a clearing in the pine forest, and bumped along for four more miles, finally pulling up in front of what was once a log cabin but which had become a fair-sized house as room after room had been added to accommodate the children that had come at two-year intervals for twenty years.

Will took one look at the emaciated man drenched with sweat and knew that he faced defeat. This was no patient with a foot to be lanced, nor someone with the spring miseries. This man had pneumonia. Even without examining Mr. Jernigan, Will saw that there was little he could do other than try to control the fever until the "crisis passed." There was so much he needed to know, and he knew so little. Will gave his patient the strongest sedative he had, prescribed a liquid diet and plenty of water, and promised to call again the next day. After following this routine every day for three weeks, Will noticed one morning that his patient was free of fever.

He was almost sure the man would recover; at the same time, he was aware he had done little.

Indeed, there was little he *could* do until the advent of sulfa drugs. "I'd rather have a case of pneumonia than a common cold," he often exclaimed in later years; "now I can treat pneumonia."

CHAPTER

3

Think You Can Handle the Fourth Grade?

Will's practice fell into a set routine. He found, however, that he had no way to spend what little leisure time he had. On rare occasions after supper, he sat on the McGaheys' screened side porch and talked with them. Since he knew nothing about local politics and was not particularly interested in the sawmilling business, conversations tended to drag. Will found it difficult to feign interest in the local supervisor's race or the growing scarcity of good stands of timber. His attention often strayed to the young lady who played the organ at the Baptist church. He wondered if she was really engaged to that doctor whose name he couldn't remember. He thought of asking Mrs. McGahey more about her but decided she might think it strange and unbecoming for him to be so much interested in a girl whose future was apparently already settled.

 The next Sunday, however, after making a couple of house calls, Will headed back to the church, the first time he had been two Sundays in a row since leaving home for medical school. He arrived just as the service was beginning and was pleased with himself at finding a seat with a clear view of Lula. He couldn't quite muster the courage to speak to her, but did manage a weak grin, and he thought there was a little movement around the corners of her mouth. Will learned that the burly, black-haired man leading the congregational singing was her brother, Felix. After the service, he waited by the front door, hoping Felix and his sister would come out together; but eventually Felix appeared alone. Deciding that a brother was better than nothing, Will went over to him and introduced himself. "So you're the new doctor I've been hearin' about," Felix replied in a rich bass voice. "I'm glad to meet you, and to know you're for real—we sure do need you. This is my brother, William," Felix added, grabbing his brother's arm. "He runs the local school, and I'd like you to meet him." "Will, I want you to meet our new doctor." Will looked into the serious gray eyes of a man as tall as he but some forty pounds lighter. "I'm glad to see you," William said.

Will thought as he returned the greeting: *I'll bet you are, because you badly need a doctor.* His next thought was: *This man has tuberculosis.* "We're having a box supper at the school Friday night, Doctor Young. We hope you can work it into your schedule."

The following week was the busiest Will had had since arriving in Boone. At midafternoon Friday, he found himself within three miles of the school—not a surprising place to be, since he had rearranged his entire schedule that day with that object in mind. He made one more call (on a patient who lived within a mile of the school) and arrived at the school just as the festivities were beginning. He wanted to be on hand when Lula brought her contribution to the auction. That way, he would be able to recognize the box when it was put up for bids. Each contestant had tried to make her box as attractive as possible (some made a special effort to make their box easily recognizable, for the same reason that occupied Will's thoughts at the moment). The purpose of this affair was to raise as much money as possible, the proceeds to go toward supplementing the school budget. A common tactic was for the boys, often with the connivance of faculty members, to spot the boxes of the girls who had regular beaus and deliberately bid up the price of the boxes.

The bidding became more vigorous when Lula's box was offered for sale. Obviously, however, it was not one of those "marked" for competition. "Doctor Haggard must not be here," Will concluded. After three or four bids, the bidding ceased, and Will knew that for seventy-five cents he would have a semi-private conversation with the pretty young organist without violating the Victorian code of conduct that governed such things in that day. When all the boxes had been sold, Will took his to find its owner. He found Lula sitting near the front, but she did not appear surprised to learn who had acquired it. (She later admitted that she had followed the bidding with interest.) "Shall we eat it here, or take it to one of the tables under the trees?" Will suggested that they take it outside. When they were seated at a table under a large oak, Will found that, to his chagrin, he didn't know how to begin a conversation. After they had both admitted they knew the other, Will asked: "Where is Doctor Haggard? I just knew he would be here."

"Oh, no," Lula said, "he has moved to the Delta and won't be back until Christmas."

What she did not tell him was that Doctor Haggard had asked her to marry him, that she had refused his offer of marriage, and that he had left the county, never to return except on brief visits.

Although for a long time their relationship moved little beyond the occasional chat about the weather, local events, and similar, impersonal matters, Will did muster enough courage to ask Lula if she would allow him to escort her to the play party to be held the next Friday at Mr. George Tucker's. She said she would. From that time until their formal engagement was announced the following December, it was difficult to determine just who was courting whom.

They were married on July 5. After the ceremony they boarded at the McGaheys' until Will could have a house built on the acre of land he had bought from Melvin Barnhill only a short distance from Barnhill's store. The young couple moved in even before the house was completed, and there they remained for fifty-five years.

Will's practice grew, as did his landholdings, until he owned more than a hundred acres and had more patients than two doctors could handle with ease. On his land he had two families who farmed on shares (half the crop to Will and half to the tenant). In addition, he had six or eight wage hands, young men who worked for six or eight dollars a month, plus room and board. Even though he at first wasn't interested, he eventually got involved in the sawmilling business. As their worldly possessions grew, so did their family. In the first fifteen years of marriage, Lula and Will had six children, five of whom lived into adulthood: Madge, Willie Grace, Myrta, Edwin, Dan, and Janey. (Will died in 1962 and Lula in 1968; Willie Grace died in infancy, and Edwin was killed in an automobile crash in 1955, at age 37; Madge died August 23, 1985, at age 76.) As the children grew up, they were often left in the care of Ma Wright, their maternal grandmother, while Lula accompanied Will to New Orleans, Meridian, or Memphis, where he was moving by train a very ill patient. They would often be away for two or three weeks at a time. Although Ma Wright never punished the children, they soon learned to obey her. Lula assured the children that if they did not behave, she would mete out punishment when she returned. That was seldom necessary. Their grandmother had a way of getting them to do what she wished done without their being fully aware that that was what she wanted. For example, when I was eight years old, she promised me that she would give me a dip of snuff if I would get some clothes from the line where they had been hung to dry. Ma Wright did as she promised, but I have never since wanted to smell another pinch of snuff. No sooner had I put a very small portion in my mouth, expecting to share Ma Wright's

Think You Can Handle the Fourth Grade? 21

obvious enjoyment when she took a dip, than my stomach began to roll. Suddenly, I saw my breakfast on the floor; and I was soon slumped down beside it. With considerable help I made my way to bed, where I remained until midafternoon. On another occasion she offered me a "dram" from the bottle of bourbon she always kept in the bottom drawer of the bureau in her room if I would run a similar errand. Again, she kept her word. But, although she mixed the bourbon with water and sugar, as she did the two drinks she had each night before retiring, it was a long time before I wanted another.

The children reached the age of six and entered the local school, which had been put together by consolidating several one-, two- and three-teacher schools. Now students could attend the same school from the first through the twelfth grades. When I was six, I enrolled in Miss Finger's room. Since the two Finger sisters taught at the same school, one was known as Little Finger and the other as Big Finger (though we didn't dare call them that to their face). I and some thirty other first- and second-graders were in Little Finger's room. It was heated by a Franklin stove, fed from a wood pile stacked outside. One of the greatest privileges a teacher could bestow was to allow one of us to help bring in the wood to be used the next day. Another was being appointed to put wood in the stove when it was needed. Still another—and possibly the most cherished of classroom assignments—was to be allowed to erase the board at the end of the day and to take the erasers outside and clean them by hitting two of them together or, if no one was watching, by slamming them against the side of the building.

In the schoolroom one grade sat in the front of the room on twelve- or fourteen-foot-long "recitation benches." The other class sat in desks at the rear of the room with instructions that they should not disturb the recitation in progress at the front of the room. The only acceptable reason for leaving one's seat was to go to the pencil sharpener. To get a drink of water from the barrel by the teacher's desk, we had to wait until the recitation was over and the position of the two grades was being exchanged. The girls had dainty little folding cups decorated with flowers and their initials, from which they drank; but most of us boys relied on tin cups our mothers used to measure ingredients when cooking. Occasionally, we constructed an unreliable, makeshift utensil by cleverly folding a sheet of paper from a Blue Horse writing tablet. As often as not, the cup would collapse and water would splash on everyone within a ten-foot radius. Then the person whose cup had failed to function properly would spend an hour or two in the dunce's corner with his back to the other pupils in the room and his nose in a ring drawn on the wall at a height to make him stand straight and strain to reach.

One of the strongest inclinations to show our fallen nature was to stack our books on the long hair of the girl sitting in the desk in front of us so that when she got up to go to the pencil sharpener or went to take her place with the scholars on the recitation benches at the front of the room, the books would hold her hair back and she would cry out. As often as not, the books would spill on the floor. One sure way to become the envy of all the boys in the room was to pull this stunt without the teacher's being aware of just what had happened.

After we reached the fourth or fifth grade, we were subjected to two kinds of punishments—either the teacher would beat our open hands with a ruler or keep us in at recess and make us memorize Bible verses or poetry. For a long time, I believed that the latter punishment caused most of us to believe that both the Bible and poetry were to be avoided.

Each morning, a large wooden barrel was filled with drinking water. All students were told repeatedly not to take more water than they could drink, that if they did, to be sure to throw the excess water out the window, *not back in the barrel*. Once, one of my classmates raised his hand and told the teacher: "Miss Slaughter,

S.B. is pouring his drinkin's back in the barrel." S.B. was carefully lectured on the dire consequences of his action, and four of the other boys were off almost half a day emptying the barrel and refilling it.

As the end of my second year of school drew near, my teacher gave me a note to take home to my mother. The note wasn't sealed, and I succumbed to curiosity and read it before I got home. (I never learned whether my mother suspected what I had done.) I attempted to act surprised the next day when I learned that my mother was going to the school and that I could ride with her in the better Model T. (My father bought a new car every year and allowed my mother to drive it for a year before he took it to make his rounds in; the two-year-old car was the one he traded in every year.) Since I had read the note, I was in a quandary as to what my reaction should be when my mother told me we wouldn't be leaving before 9:30, two hours after the school bus usually stopped at the front gate.

She took no special notice of my reaction, however. We arrived at the school and went directly to Superintendent McGahey's office, where we were soon joined by my teacher, Miss Slaughter, and another woman I knew only by sight. I was still struggling with the problem of what reaction to use, and only by the greatest effort was managing to contain my emotions. With Mr. McGahey's first question, though, I smiled from ear to ear.

"Dan," Mr. McGahey asked, "do you think you can handle the fourth grade?" He was asking, of course, Do you want to skip the third grade? My throat filled and I couldn't speak; but I vigorously pumped my head up and down. "I don't know if that's a good idea," my mother said. Then she turned to me. "You'll be leaving all your friends; and besides, I've heard the third grade is the most important one in grammar school." My mind was running over the roster of this year's third grade and next year's fourth grade, wondering if I knew as many boys in the third as I did the second when Mr. McGahey said: "I wouldn't worry about Dan making friends in the fourth grade. He'll do fine. Miss Slaughter, Miss Scott (the fourth-grade teacher), and I have studied Dan's record carefully, and we're convinced he can do the work. In fact, we believe that his taking the third grade would be a waste of time." After a moment's silence, my mother said: "It's Dan's decision." Then she turned to me: "Do you want to skip the third? Do you think you can do fourth-grade work? You'll have to study hard."

Despite every effort, I couldn't utter a word. Finally I managed a "Sure!" As I said this, I glanced at Miss Scott, who had her arms open wide. I went to her and she hugged me tight. Little did I know that I was about to enter one of the most exciting, interesting, and important years of my grammar-school career.

My life, of course, wasn't taken up entirely with school. Living, as I did, within walking distance of the families of three of my mother's brothers and two of her sisters, there was a lot of visiting back and forth. Almost every Sunday one of the families would accompany my family and me from church for dinner and often stay until evening service. Soon after dinner, my brother and sisters and I would invite the cousins down to the barn to play, usually hide-and-seek, though there were others: tag, ring-around-the-rosie, handkerchief, come-over. These games were unsupervised, but one of the adults would peep out occasionally to check on us, that is, to make sure no one was fighting. Except for an occasional flare of temper when one of the hiders would accuse the one who was "it" of peeping, things went smoothly. In fact, the manifestation of good feeling was so pervasive that when I was about ten I was so terribly embarrassed to be kissed by my eleven-year-old cousin, who happened to be hiding with me, that I gave myself up, though the last thing I wanted to be was "it."

Besides Sunday visits, the families moved freely from one house to another "sitting each other till bedtime." On these occasions, if it was summer, the adults would sit on the porch and talk, or, if winter, in the living room, or parlor, and the children would make candy (usually molasses) or popcorn balls, after which we would play games. We'd play handkerchief or cross-questions and crooked-answers or heavy, heavy hangs over your head—Is it fine or superfine? (Fine was for a boy and superfine, a girl.) When it was determined which sex *it* was, that person was assigned a menial task such as "Bring in some more wood" or "Bring me a popcorn ball." Or one might be asked to do something slightly embarrassing, such as "Waltz around the room" or "Do the Charleston." As for myself, I'd rather have had fifty lashes with my father's razor strap than attempt to do any of these adult dances. Not only was it silly, it was embarrassing, because I couldn't dance. But, then, neither could anyone else. While the younger children were engaged in such games, the older boys and girls would listen to the Gramaphone. Some of the older ones were even trying to learn to dance—usually two boys or two girls forming a couple and watching their feet as they tried to force them through unfamiliar, sometimes intricate maneuvers. All of the children, including me after I entered junior high school, regularly attended the parties given somewhere in the community at least once a week. There, the games—Post Office, Spin-the-Bottle, and I Wish—were intended to establish a relationship between boys and girls. Sometimes even a little dancing was allowed, though it was usually clogging or square dancing. Round dancing, in which the boy puts his arms around the girl and she puts hers around him, was seldom permitted. Sometimes the party was announced as a "candy-pulling," which meant that making and eating molasses candy was to be the principal activity and that the games, if any, were secondary. Often the adults would act as chaperones sitting in one room and talking while the children played next door. Through these parties, as well as spelling bees and church activities, most of us were thrown together several times each week.

Spelling bees were held each Friday afternoon in almost all of the elementary grades. They provided opportunities for the teacher to demonstrate how much her pupils were learning. If a room contained two grades—say, the fifth and sixth—each grade had a spelling bee on alternate Fridays. The manner in which the class to be tested was divided into equal groups varied. Sometimes the teacher would make the division, trying to put the same number of good spellers in each group. At other times, she would select the best two spellers in the room and allow them to choose those they wanted on their side.

The contest followed a simple pattern: The teacher would invite a qualified member of the community to be the spelling master, providing him with a list of words the class had studied. The pupils would line up on two sides in the recitation area at the front of the room. The class not participating on a particular afternoon and visiting parents would sit in the regular seating area—folding chairs were always available to accommodate an overflow crowd. The spelling master would pronounce a word from the list the teacher had given him and ask the person at the head of one of the lines to spell it. If the student spelled the word correctly, the spelling master would choose another word and ask the student at the head of the other line to try. When that student misspelled a word, he or she had to sit down, and the word was given to the student at the head of the other line. So the game proceeded.

At one of these Friday-afternoon spelling bees, presided over by Edgar Barnhill (who now worked in the Louisville post office), I was one of the last two participants standing. The word I was asked to spell was *soot,* and I spelled it exactly as it had been pronounced. But Edgar pronounced the word "sut," although Miss

Scott had been careful to pronounce it "soot." That was wrong, Edgar said, and I was told to sit down.

Miss Scott prepared us for the public spelling bees by holding private ones several times a week. In one of these matches, I remembered, she had asked someone to spell the word *yellow,* and the boy had responded: "yaller, spells y-a-l-l-e-r.") "No," Miss Scott said, "not *yaller.* It is yeller; y-e-l-l-o-w. Remember—the second letter is an *e.*" (In those days, too, we said *winder* and *sparrer* for *window* and *sparrow.*) At these practice sessions, one did not *sit down* for a misspelled word; he or she was "turned down." The one who spelled a word correctly moved around each of those who missed it, toward the head of the line. One afternoon the word *squirrel* was given and everyone missed it until it came the turn of Whit Hill, a notoriously bad speller. For weeks, Whit had been at the foot of the line every time at the end of a match. This time, he knew, he wouldn't have to suffer that indignity. He took one step forward and said in a loud, confident voice: "*Squirrel. Squee-U-R-L,* and up to the head I go, by God." Whit's punishment was not confined to being "turned down." He was turned down in a different, more literal way, with a paddle being applied to his posterior.

Every summer, the principal of Bond School went to Peabody College in Nashville, to work on his master's degree. There he learned about I.Q. tests and decided that all the students in the seventh grade through the twelfth should have an I.Q. test. He would then put the results in the students' records, and the information could be used, or so he had been assured at Peabody, to get a better idea of how close to a student's capacity he or she was achieving. The only time he could schedule a test was on a Saturday morning. One can imagine our reaction when we learned that we would have to give up a Saturday morning to take a test that would not count on our grades. But the principal insisted. He even announced in assembly that anyone not present for the test would have to bring a legitimate excuse from his family on Monday.

At nine o'clock on the announced Saturday, almost everyone was there. The questions were multiple choice; the student had to choose the best answer to a question from four possibilities. After about two hours of intense effort—some of the questions were very difficult—I walked out into the front yard as soon as the teacher called time. There, some of my friends joined me. "Doc [by now, my nickname], what did you do on that first one?" one of them asked. (Which of the following names does not belong in this series? (a) Mary (b) Jane (c) Tom (d) Emma.)

"I answered *Tom* because he was the only boy in the group."

"My God, I said *Emma*," my friend replied in disgust. He's still called "Little Emma" by those who know him.

Sunday School and church were the big social events of the week. There were two churches in the community—Baptist and Methodist. Baptist services were on Sunday morning and evening, and Methodist Sunday School, with preaching on alternate Sundays, was in the afternoon. At about nine-thirty, the Model T bus that ordinarily served as a school bus would come by the house, and we would pile in and go to the services at the Baptist church. Each of us carried a Bible, because we knew we would be graded by our Sunday School teacher and the results would be posted on a big board kept in the alcove outside the sanctuary:

BROUGHT BIBLE (10)
ON TIME (10)
PRESENT LAST SUNDAY (10)
DRESS [coat and tie in winter, tie in summer] (10)
PARTICIPATION IN CLASS DISCUSSION (10)
STUDIED LESSON (50)

Those who earned ninety or more points received a gold star, which was placed after their names on the board. Those with

Think You Can Handle the Fourth Grade? 29

eighty to ninety points got a silver star; and those with fifty to eighty points received a bronze star. To receive any score at all, however, we had to make a contribution to the church. Those who received a gold star every Sunday for three months were given a New Testament with their name embossed in gold on the cover. Those who earned a gold star every Sunday for a year were given a Bible, complete with the Apocrypha between the Old and New testaments.

I managed only one Bible in eight years, though I earn several testaments. It seemed that almost every fall, I came down with mumps or measles or whooping cough or some other childhood disease.

After every question the Sunday School teacher asked, nearly every one of the ten or twelve students in the room would have their hands up, shaking them vigorously trying to attract the teacher's attention. But she nearly always asked a girl for the answer. Only if the answer given was unsatisfactory would she ask one of us boys. Occasionally an unprepared scholar would be caught attempting to deceive the teacher and bluff through the answer. The chance of being found out was so great that we usually were afraid to raise our hand unless we were sure we knew the answer. *What was Jesus' mother's name? What sea did the Chosen People cross on their way to the Promised Land? Did they cross just one? Out of what did God speak to Moses?*

After Sunday School, families met and sat together in the sanctuary for the fervently delivered hour-and-a-half sermon. Following that, the minister would "open the doors of the church," inviting the unsaved to accept the Lord and join the church so they could receive God's mercy and grace and (most of all) salvation on Judgment Day. After the sermon and several repeated invitations, the last hymn would be sung and the minister would dismiss the congregation.

My family and I usually joined one or more of the aunts and

uncles and their families for dinner (at that time, the midday meal). As soon as we entered the house, we knew what the wife of the house had been doing most of the previous week. The aroma of cooked and cooking food was almost overpowering. In summer, the black husband of the cook would likely be turning the handle of a freezer of ice cream in the backyard. We children would pause on the back porch just long enough to pull our shoes off. Then we would head for the barn for games before dinner. As we raced down the back steps, we would hear: "If you get your Sunday clothes dirty, I'm gonna skin you alive." Paying little attention to this threat, we would run with seemingly inexhaustible energy until we heard "Dinner's ready!" coming from the house. We hurried into the dining room and found a place at the fourteen-foot-long table and, as Uncle Tom would always say, "fed our faces." As soon as we had finished, we went to the mirror on the porch to try to repair the damage done to our appearance by the games and the eating. It was time for the Wrights to pile into my mother's car (my father would have come in his own car in order to "make a call in Possum Hollow") and go to New Hope, the Methodist church for Sunday School and, if it was a second or fourth Sunday, for preaching. Then it was back home, where preparations were immediately begun for BYPU and another sermon at Murphy Creek Baptist Church. Although the service did not begin until seven, we had to leave early, since we would be traveling by mule-drawn wagon. The Barnhill boys would come by and pick up the Wrights and the Youngs, then other groups at other houses. Soon the wagon was full, and the courting couples would get out and walk, deliberately letting the wagon get farther and farther ahead until it was almost out of sight. As the wagon neared the church, this procedure would be reversed, and they would increase their pace until they had practically caught up with the wagon.

After BYPU—which was much like Sunday School, except that BYPU was more social and all the young people met together—and another long sermon, all the young people from Boone would pile in the wagon for the three-mile trek home. Again, the courting couples fell behind as the wagon slowly jolted over the rutted roads. When the wagon reached Murphy Creek swamp, no one could be seen in the inky darkness behind the wagon, and when it had passed through the swamp and was approaching Boone, it would stop, the driver well aware that the parents of those who had left home on the wagon would expect them to be on the wagon when it returned. Sometimes the wagon waited thirty minutes.

The church offered other opportunities for getting together. Each summer an itinerant singing master came to Murphy Creek Church to offer a week-long opportunity for instruction and practice in "shape-note" singing, the system of determining the time and pitch of a song by the shape of the note. Primarily because it was simple, this technique, also known as "sacred harp" or "fosola," was popular throughout the South in the late nineteenth and early twentieth centuries. One could quickly learn to read music.

The Sunday the minister announced the dates of the singing school, every adolescent in the community began to plan his or her schedule so that nothing would interfere with attending every session of the school. If just one meeting was missed, the boy or girl would be "behind" the others. Equally important was the fact that if the participant were absent only a few times, he or she wouldn't be assigned to one of the special groups that performed at the all-day singing which always came at the conclusion of the singing school. Even worse, someone else might take a certain place beside a certain someone. During the entire week, that someone was a constant companion—they talked during the brief recesses, shared their sack lunches, and walked home together if they lived in the same direction from the church. (I had fifteen cows to milk every afternoon, so I couldn't waste much time when school was dismissed for the day.) If everything went smoothly, I attempted to establish a relationship that would carry over into the next school year.

One of the touchstones of my youth—for many years, I could measure my emotional state by comparing my present feeling with how I felt on that occasion—was the time I was chosen to sing tenor in the mixed quartet (two girls, two boys) that would perform at the all-day singing. Being chosen a member of one of the two or three quartets was the highest honor one could receive at the school; the only other special assignments were to the men's or women's choruses.

The song selected for the quartet to sing was "They Crucified My Savior." I couldn't sing very well (I was often accused of being "unable to carry a tune in a sack"), but I listened carefully as the singing master showed me how my part should sound and by midweek could imitate a competent singer almost exactly. When our turn came on Sunday, just before the congregation was dismissed for lunch, I opened my mouth wide just as I had been instructed to do and, I thought, sang beautifully my part. I was confirmed in that impression when Miss Scott said as I stepped down from the platform: "Why, Dan, I didn't know you could sing tenor. You're good, really good!" Although I escorted the young lady I had been standing next to all week and who had sung soprano in the quartet through the food line and heaped my plate with fried chicken, country cured ham, assorted fresh vegetables, and caramel pie, for the only time I could remember I did not know what I was eating or what the young lady and I were saying. I didn't want to eat or talk; I wanted to sing.

CHAPTER

4

Lula, that New Car of Yours Has Bad Habits

As the nation moved deeper into the Great Depression, more and more farmland became available. Few people in the Boone community had enough money to pay their taxes, not to mention what they had borrowed from the local bank for fertilizer and seed while they made a crop. My father often bought land adjoining or near his land at a reasonable price, which allowed the seller to avoid foreclosure.

Soon his holdings were considerable. One year, he planted more than a hundred acres of cotton, in addition to corn, hay, sorghum, vegetables, and other crops. It was a common practice for a farmer who owed a bill to stop by the house and tell my mother who had come to the front door: "Tell Doc I put a load of corn in his crib." Or: "If an old brown cow with a crooked right horn comes up with his'n tonight, tell him I turned it in his pasture." What bookkeeping was done was informal. Neither my father nor his patients had a clear idea of their indebtedness.

One day I went with my father to the courthouse. He was going to pay his taxes. Crossing the street, we met Mr. Deck Fair, owner of the town's largest sawmill. It was also about the only industry in town.

"Doc, I hear you've been seeing some of my people." (He meant the mill workers and their families.)

"That's right," my father replied.

"Well, how much do I owe you?"

With no more than a second's pause, my father replied: "Eighty-four dollars," whereupon the other man reached in his pocket and took out an impressive roll of bills and counted out the money. Mr. Fair never asked which of his people my father had seen, nor did he ask for a receipt. What a trusting, gentlemanly way to do business, I thought. Later, I wondered: How will the man get his money back—prorate it among the workers? Raise the price of lumber? Lower everyone's wages? Or merely absorb the loss?

Whichever method was used, the system was a highly paternalistic one. Only the owner decided how he was going to cover the doctor's bills for those working under him. When the owner died a few years later, his heirs sold the mill to a conglomerate which converted the mill to manufacture low-cost processed wall board.

I was indifferent to work on the farm, but my father insisted that everyone do his bit. Therefore, at sunup each day, I was sent to the field with a hoe to weed cotton or corn. As soon as my father left for his office or to call on a patient, I would busily work at my hoeing until he was out of sight; then I would find the nearest tree, lean up against it, and take a *Wild West Weekly* from under my shirt and begin reading.

Often I would continue reading until I heard the dinner bell, which sounded at 11:30. When the bell rang, the workers who were plowing would unhitch the mules from the plow, ride them to the barn, remove their harness, and water and feed them before going on to the house. Those who were hoeing or clearing brush would put their tools in the shade and walk to the house and rest on the porch or under the shade of a tree until the plowmen finished caring for their mules and came to the house. Then everyone would wash up at the well before going to the house for a huge midday meal of fried chicken, ham, three or four fresh vegetables, and blackberry or peach cobbler pie. The table, at least eight feet in diameter, would easily seat twelve people and was in two tiers. Plates were set on the bottom tier and the food on the top. Each man would serve himself from the dish in front of him while the cook, waving a peach-tree switch over the table to shoo flies away, rotated the top tier so everyone could serve himself. As soon as a dish was about half-empty, the cook would call to her husband in the kitchen to bring more bread or peas or milk. When everyone had eaten his fill, all hands would tramp out to the front porch and nap until the bell rang again at one, indicating that it was time to return to the fields, where they would remain until sundown.

One afternoon I was sitting with my back against a small oak tree, reading, my hoe lying at my feet. I was deeply absorbed in a *Wild West Weekly* story. There was a loud bang, and the tree shook so hard that I dropped my magazine. My first thought was that the tree had been struck by lightning. But the sun was shining brightly. Then I turned and saw my father walking away. He was carrying an axe on his shoulder and was already some distance away. I knew what had happened. I returned to weeding corn, and from then on my reading was confined to nights, Saturday afternoons, and Sundays. My father had accomplished his purpose; he never considered it necessary to mention the Incident of the Youth and the Ax.

One Sunday morning when I was fifteen, my father came in to breakfast and announced to my mother: "Lula, that new car of yours has bad habits. I know it smokes because I saw cigarette butts all over the floor and on the seats. If it ever starts to drinking, I'm going to get rid of it."

No one spoke. The meal continued as though my father hadn't said a word on the subject. But my brother and I, who had used the car the night before, were careful thereafter to clean it thoroughly before coming home.

By the time I was twelve my father had given Edwin and me an acre of cotton for our own. It was near the kitchen garden. He always referred to it as his "brag patch"; Edwin and I claimed it as our 4-H Club project. Every spring my father had the manure from the cow barn spread on the patch, and he put twice as much commercial fertilizer on that acre as he did on any other on the place. As he often said, "I aim to make two bales of cotton on that one acre," an intention Edwin and I agreed wholeheartedly with. Usually Edwin would plow the patch and I would weed it—not a small undertaking, since the vast amount of fertilizer used on that one acre made the grass and cockle burrs thrive; they seemed to grow six inches every night.

When the cotton was mature, Edwin and I would pick it, load it on a wagon, and take it to the gin. The latter job had to be done on Friday afternoon. We had to wait our turn, and usually there were from ten to thirty wagons waiting to move onto the platform. If we went at any other time, we'd be late for school. After the cotton was ginned, Edwin and I would sell the seed to the ginner to pay for the ginning. Usually the price of the seed would exceed the cost of the ginning by ten or twelve dollars. The ginner would give us a small amount of the cotton, called a sample. The bale would be given a number, a copy of which would be attached to the sample along with a statement indicating how much the bale of cotton weighed. Edwin and I would then take the sample and hitch a ride, usually with someone else going to the cotton buyer's. There, without any help from a grown-up, we would sell our bale of cotton. When it had been sold, we would go over to my father's office and report to him how much the bale weighed and the price it brought. Counting the money for the seed, we usually had between forty and fifty dollars left, at a time when a grown man received no more than a dollar for a full day's labor on the farm.

My father never asked for the money nor questioned the twelve- and fourteen-year old boys how we intended to spend it. We always went over to Fair Company's or to Stubbs', two of the most popular stores in town, and bought school clothes. Once we bought a sweater, a cap, two pairs of shoes, and five pairs of cotton trousers with matching shirts. For the next three weeks, by matching or mixing the sets of shirts and trousers, Edwin was able to wear a different suit of clothing to school every day. This feat was so unusual at the little country school he and I attended—where many boys wore the same suit of overalls for a week, had it washed on Saturday, and wore it again the next week—that the school wit remarked Edwin looked like some rich man's poodle dog. A version of the name stuck, and for the rest of his life Edwin was known as "Pedoodlum."

Milking some sixteen cows was another of our responsibilities. This duty soon became a nuisance. Every morning we had to get up in time to milk (I was the better milker, so I milked nine or ten cows every morning and afternoon and Edwin only five or six). After milking, we had to carry the milk to the house, get the milk we had collected the night before (left in lard pails in the well overnight to keep it from souring), separate the cream from the milk, and put the cream on a stand near the highway, where the creamery truck would pick it up. Then we had to bathe (not too well), dress, and eat breakfast before the school bus—in the fall and spring, the school wagon in the winter—arrived. Perhaps the greatest imposition came in the spring and summer when we had to leave in the middle of a baseball game (actually, stick ball) to get home and milk. On the other hand, we received regular income from selling the cream. We would split the weekly check with our mother, who used her part as spending money and to buy clothing for the girls.

Each summer of my childhood, the high point was our visit to my grandma and grandpa in New Augusta, a village about two hundred miles away. We left at daylight, my youngest sister, Janey, sitting in the front seat with Father and Mother, and Madge, Myrta, Edwin, and I on the back seat. Occasionally the fighting for window seats on the back seat became so noisy that my father couldn't concentrate on his driving well enough to miss the many potholes in the road or to negotiate properly the numerous hairpin curves. When his nerves had suffered enough, he would allow my brother and me to ride on the fenders of the car until we were so tired we would sit quietly between our two older sisters, who were so glad to have an unobstructed view that they would sometimes let us go to sleep with our heads on their shoulders.

Our aim at the outset was to get as far as Bay Springs (about seventy-five miles) by twelve o'clock, so we could eat the lunch my mother had packed and wash it down with water from the artesian well. Then we would try to reach Ellisville (about eighty more miles) by nightfall and sleep there in the hotel after feasting on liverwurst (which my father called liver cheese) and bologna placed between two slices of loaf bread, or light bread, as we called it. This feast was accompanied by a bottle of "sody water." My mother wouldn't drink Coca-Cola nor allow us to do so, because she thought it contained "dope" (a popular name for the drink at the time).

Even though we always began these journeys in a virtually new car (my father always waited until just before the trip to buy a new one), the roads were so rutted and dusty that we had great difficulty meeting even this unambitious schedule. If we ran into a hole, as we almost always did, and burst a tire, we might not get to Ellisville until the big grocery store there was closed, and we would have to take whatever we could get. The sleeping arrangements were dictated by the daytime seating arrangements in the car: front-seat passengers slept in one room, and back-seat passengers in the other.

We would leave early and be in Runnelstown by ten o'clock, where we stretched our legs, drank some artesian water, and had a

Moon Pie at Mr. Runnel's store. Then we were off, reaching my grandparents' by lunchtime.

First, we would drop Madge and Myrta off at Aunt Sadie's, my father's sister, who had girls about their age. Then Edwin and I would get off at Aunt Mary's, another sister, with sons our age. My father, mother, and Janey went on to grandma's and grandpa's. There we made headquarters for three or four weeks, although, after about a week, my father, mother, and Janey would return home.

After Father and Mother left, we boys would visit our grandparents every day. Grandpa had rented most of his large farm to a neighbor but reserved about five acres for fruit trees, grapes, pumpkins, peanuts, watermelons, and various vegetables. Well into his late seventies, Grandpa personally cared for these crops. Every afternoon in season, he would bring the watermelons that were ripe and put them on the back porch. When Edwin and I visited, which was every morning and afternoon, he would allow us to choose the melons we wished to cut. These daily visits we never missed.

Grandpa and Grandma had very different manners and beliefs. A religious woman, my grandmother attended every service and meeting at the local Baptist church. One of her friends told me that every time the door of the church opened, it was opened by Henrietta. She prepared no food between sundown Saturday and daybreak Monday. She would not eat the eggs the hens laid on Sunday, instead she would sell them and give the money to the church.

My grandfather, a man of less temperate habits, began every day with a couple of long pulls at the jug of moonshine he kept under his bed. After breakfast, he would go out on the front porch and try to hit a four-by-eight-inch hole he had made by removing pieces of board from the floor with the amber from a large slab of Brown's Mule chewing tobacco which he constantly shifted from jaw to jaw. His only other activity most mornings was glancing through the paper and telling any available grandchild of the old days "up in Kemper County," where one often saw panthers and something he called "catty-meows" (by which he may have meant wildcats). In deference to Grandma's feelings, he watched the time closely and just before she called lunch, he would carefully scrub the area around the hole carefully with sand and splash two or three buckets of water on it.

Jack and Jimmie usually accompanied us home. Jimmie and I could find enough to keep us busy playing hide-and-seek or jump-the-rope with other children in the neighborhood; but Jack and Edwin were so constantly in pursuit of the opposite sex that my father's observation that they would have a "stable full of girls" when they grew up turned out to be an understatement. When they had stayed as long as they could, usually a week before school was to begin, my father allowed Edwin and me to take them halfway home in the Model A Ford we had acquired when Edwin was sixteen and I was fourteen. Somewhere around Stringer, we would meet Uncle Jim and Aunt Mary. For Edwin and me, this trip was the climax of the summer. So great was our excitement that we forgot for a few hours that school would soon begin.

When I was about fifteen, I discovered that my father was a clever psychologist. Farming on the place was done by two kinds of laborers—sharecropper, or tenant, and wage hand. Some sharecroppers worked for a share of what they grew. If a man provided for himself and his family, furnished his stock and plow tools, he would give my father one-fourth of the cotton and one-third of the corn he produced. If he furnished nothing but his labor, with my father supplying everything else, they divided equally what the tenant produced. The farmer was allowed to keep a vegetable garden and milk one of my father's cows. Both kinds of tenants worked pretty much as they chose, with occasional advice from my father.

The other type of laborer was different. My father usually had two or three wage hands whom he paid eight or ten dollars a month, plus room and board. These laborers worked directly under his supervision; but my father, whose medical practice was more than a full-time job and who also operated two small sawmills with the assistance of a supervisor, had little time to devote to a farm with over two hundred acres under cultivation. Many weeks he was at home only a few hours between 10:00 in the evening and 4:00 in the morning.

He called me aside one day and said: "These wage hands aren't going to work any harder than you do. I'm counting on you."

Until the ground was broken and seeds planted, there was no real problem. Everyone was plowing; and twice in the morning and twice in the afternoon, Edwin would send me to the spring for water. Everyone continued plowing until I returned. Then I would go to each in turn and wait until he came to the end of the row. Then the plowman would stop his mule, turn around, lean heavily on the plow stock and drink deeply from the jar of water I had brought; then he would roll a cigarette out of Bull Durham or Country Gentleman tobacco, take a few deep drags, and flip it away. After the cotton and corn was up, however, the situation changed drastically. Since Edwin and one other hand could do all the plowing, the rest of us began thinning the cotton or corn and digging the grass and weeds from the drill where it was growing. This was a slow, tedious process because it was all done with a hoe. The regular hands and I couldn't do all the hoeing at the time it needed to be done, so my father often sent a truck to the "quarters" each morning at daylight to pick up twelve to fifteen black men or women who would be paid about sixty cents for a twelve-hour work day. Each night before the extra hoe hands were to arrive the next morning, he would impress on me the importance of my duties: "You must set the pace for twelve or fifteen people. They will go no faster than you. They will sit down every time you do. Find the slowest worker in the group and appoint him water boy, and send him for water three or four times a day. Watch the other workers. See that they leave the correct number of stalks in each hill and that they chop down the grass and weeds." He was so persuasive that I hoed as fast and as carefully as I could. The *Wild West Weekly* stories were relegated to nights (unless I was too tired) and weekends.

Almost every Saturday afternoon or evening, depending upon the other demands on our time, Edwin and I would go into town to the "picture show." Twenty-five cents paid our admission, bought a Barq's root-beer, a Power House candy bar, a bag of popcorn, a double-feature, and a serial. The serial usually ended with the heroine tied to the railroad tracks and a train approaching at ninety miles an hour or with the hero mounted on a horse with a noose around his neck, the other end of the rope tied to the limb of a tree, while a leering villain in a black hat had a whip poised to hit the horse. Although we knew everything would turn out all right, and repeatedly told each other so during the next week, we could hardly wait from one Saturday to the next.

Every day, Barkstol Shaw, who had been wounded in World War I, walked past the house on his way to town, where he would spend an eight- or ten-hour shift sitting on one of the benches in front of the courthouse, whittling and talking to anyone else with the leisure to spend part of a workday listening to Barkstol's war experiences. One afternoon just before sundown, he came down the road from town and headed toward his home three miles away on the far side of Possum Hollow. He drew even with our front gate, then saw my father and me sitting on the side porch in the shade. As he walked up to the front steps, my father whispered: "He's going to try to get a ride home." Getting home, however, wasn't the only thing—or maybe not the principal thing—on Barkstol's mind. After some pleasantries and idle comments on the weather, he frowned and said: "Doc, the darnest thing happened to me today." My father, knowing that Barkstol was going to tell him what had happened, made no comment.

This morning I was a settin' on the banch in front of the courthouse and I looked over on the other banch and I seen a man I thought I knowed. After a spell I looked back over there an' seen he was a lookin' at me, and I thought that he thought he knowed me. I just kept on whittlin' but in a while I looked back over there and I thought that he knowed that he thought he knowed me and I knowed that I thought that I knowed him so we got up and started toward each other. We met and of all the huggin' and back-slappin' you ever seen, we done it. After a little we turned each other aloose and stood there about two foot apart, each one eyeballin' the other, and you know what, Doc? *It wadn't neither one of us.*

With a straight face, my father looked at Barkstol and said: "I'm sorry you were disappointed." "Awh, that's all right," Barkstol replied; "no harm done. We set down and got acquainted." I wanted to laugh, but Barkstol had such a serious expression on his face that I was afraid he might be offended.

When I was in college years later, and read tales in the tradition of Old Southwest humor, I knew I had heard stories worthy of Sut Livingood himself. I was acquainted with the tradition when I first read Faulkner's "Spotted Horses," "A Fool About A Horse," and "Was." Nor did it take much imagination to know what Eudora Welty is doing in "Why I Live at the P.O." or *The Ponder Heart*.

Finally, Barkstol said, "It's gittin' late and I better go on home and feed up everythang." "It *is* late" my father replied; "and if you're going to get there before dark, you'd better let me take you."

Speaking as though such a courtesy had never occurred to him, Barkstol said: "That's right thoughty of you, Doc."

CHAPTER

5

Listen to Leon

I entered the seventh grade and was transferred from the grammar school (grades one through six) to the high school (seven through twelve). This transfer represented a significant change in my school life. When the bell rang for "books," I didn't line up before my classroom door—one line for boys and one for girls. Unless the roads were muddy and the truck got stuck, as it did with considerable frequency in winter, when I arrived at school about 7:45, I went directly to the seat that had been assigned to me in the study hall and left my books, then to the playground until the bell rang. There was no more lining up; I went directly to my seat. Every day opened with a short devotional, usually conducted by the principal, which might be followed by a short program by one of the classes. Once a week, the grammar school was invited to share high school "chapel." On those days, one of the grammar-school classes would have the program consisting of a devotional, recitations by some of the students in the room presenting the program, and a short prayer. When I was in the sixth grade, my sister, Myrta, was valedictorian of the senior class. She had ordered a valedictory speech from a company that specialized in providing speeches, class rings, and diplomas. Every afternoon she would memorize part of the speech, and that evening she tried to repeat aloud what she had memorized while my mother or Madge held the paper and prompted her. Although I never held the paper, I listened every evening as she practiced; consequently, I came to know the speech as well as she did. One day it was raining, and my class had to stay inside. I was amusing some of my friends by repeating my sister's valedictory address: "Parents, teachers, classmates, and friends: Some of us come here this evening for the last time, but whether we go or stay, we shall have ample causes to remember this institution with gratitude. . . ." I continued in this vein until I had completed the speech. My teacher overheard me and was so impressed that she asked if I would give the oration in chapel. So, the next day, I stood up and gave—word for word, complete with proper emphases and pauses—the mail-order valedictory speech my sister was to give only two weeks hence.

One can well imagine the reception I got at home that afternoon was not cool but cold. If my mother had carried out her threat to skin me alive—and I was afraid she might—my situation would have been even more precarious. At least I learned never to do such a foolish thing again.

In high school I had not one teacher but one for each subject. Rather than sit in the back of the room while another grade recited, I spent my nonclass periods in study hall. I had only four classes—English, history, mathematics, and science—which meant that I had three free periods a day. During those periods, students in study hall were supervised either by a teacher without a scheduled class or by the principal. We were allowed considerably more freedom than we had enjoyed in grammar school. We could quietly consult a classmate about an assignment or go to the library to use a dictionary, encyclopedia, or some other reference book; the library, supervised by the English teacher when she wasn't teaching class, usually was unattended. If she happened to be in, one could check out a library book. Some of the more adventuresome students would even browse through the stacks when she was absent.

The quality of instruction we received varied widely from subject to subject and from year to year. It wasn't until years later that I realized I had received my best instruction in mathematics, algebra, and plane geometry. Instruction in science was, except for a period of two years, at best average. The rest of the time, science instruction was left to two men, both of whom were concurrently pastor of the local Baptist church. To them, the teaching of science was a convenient way to deflect a potential threat to revealed religion. Usually, history and social studies were taught casually by whoever happened to be basketball coach. As a player, I and the others who played expected preferential treatment, for the coach's mind was usually on the upcoming game. The best and most demanding classes I had were those during the tenure of Coach Mapp (also the best coach I had in high school).

My English teacher for the seventh through the twelfth grades was the same person. She knew after the second year that she didn't have to tolerate a comma fault or subject-verb disagreements from me—and she did not. She knew the quality of work of which I was capable and would accept nothing less. Her justification for demanding more of me than she did of some of the other students was often expressed in a statement such as: "You'll be expected to know this or to write correctly when you go to college."

Once I tried to give a book report on *The Campfire Girls' Trip Up The River*. I was fascinated by what I considered a pun in the title—how could girls "trip up" a river? I wrote in my first sentence: "Did they place logs in the river, divert its flow, and create a 'fall' as a football player does when he 'trips up' a member of the opposing team?" Despite this attempt at cleverness, my teacher knew I was wasting my time and hers reporting on such a book in the tenth grade; so, when I had read enough to give her the drift, she said: "That's enough, Dan. You may sit down."

I sat there humiliated and seething for the remainder of the hour, at the end of which she called me by her desk. Giving me a three-by-five card, she said: "Here are the books that you are to report on for the remainder of the year." I looked at the titles on the card: *David Copperfield, Les Miserables, Oliver Twist, Vanity Fair, Pride and Prejudice, Jane Eyre*. It wasn't until I was in college and exempt from freshman English that I realized what a well-qualified, sensitive, and interested tutor I had had. There were never more than ten students in each class. The teacher, who knew precisely what each student was capable of, insisted that students perform at the highest level they were capable of.

The school I attended had only six in my graduating class. Most professional educators would probably declare such a school an inferior one. In hindsight, though, Bond School had some advantages over larger schools. It had some disadvantages, too, for example, in the choice of courses. Because I was taking the college preparatory course, I was required to take two years of Latin, whereas those who intended to get a job immediately took typing and courses in agriculture, business, home economics, and so forth.

Although I had played basketball since I was in the seventh grade, I didn't try out for the varsity team until I was in the tenth. Much to my surprise, I made the squad and played in the latter stages of interscholastic matches, after the outcome of a game had pretty much been decided. I didn't enjoy that year of basketball. The practice sessions and the games I participated in were little different from the pick-up games I had engaged in for several years. The coach, who taught science and was a Baptist minister, knew little about coaching and *did* little except toss the ball up to begin practice and blow his whistle when some player committed an obvious (and usually disabling) foul. There was no semblance of team play; each player merely tried to control the ball and thus dominate the game.

In my junior year, everything was different. Coach Mapp had played basketball at one of the state junior colleges and let everyone know who was in charge. "All right!" he yelled at us when we reported for practice. "Two hundred laps around the court!" As the last one straggled back, he yelled again: "All right! Everybody on his feet." We could barely move, but somehow everyone made it onto the court, where Coach Mapp lined the squad up facing one direction. "Run as fast as you can. When I blow the whistle, turn and run as fast as you can in the other direction." After about ten minutes of this drill, fewer than half the squad could still move, and even they were walking. The others lay where they had fallen, exhausted. Those who could still stand, and the few who could rise to their feet were taken to the foul lines and told to shoot fifty free shots. Five men shot at each basket and the others retrieved the balls and passed them back to the shooters, while the coach alternated between the two baskets, demonstrating the proper procedure of throwing the ball toward the basket and insisting that everyone follow in excruciating detail the procedure he had demonstrated.

After this first practice, the squad dropped from thirty-five to twenty-two, and two weeks later it was down to fourteen. Then Coach Mapp began installing his patterned offense and defense: a high-low post offense and a three-two zone defense. It had never occurred to us, even those who had played for several years, that basketball was such an organized sport. Still, we wondered when the preliminaries would be finished and we could *play* ball. Little did we realize that these weren't merely preliminaries but an explanation of the way we would play the game from then on. If one wanted to be taken out of a game, all he had to do was fail to be in his assigned position at the right time. The player who made two mistakes in quick succession knew he would play no more that game. The team had a 22–5 record and went to the finals in the regional tournament; but for me the high point of the season came the afternoon I scored eighteen points in a 25–14 victory over the school's archrival. The lead sentence in that week's edition of the school paper read: "Thursday it was Richardson [a guard] to Hull [the other forward] to Young and two points."

In addition to box suppers, fiddlers' contests, spelling bees, dramatic productions, and meetings of the Parent-Teacher Association, two other means by which the school tended to unify the community were parents' nights and community meetings. Four of five times each semester, any interested parent could come to the school and find out just what his child was studying and how well he or she was doing. Any parent could go through his child's schedule, moving from room to room, just as his child did each day, listening to the teacher explain exactly what she was trying to teach the children and discussing their progress. There were always samples of written work and copies of textbooks and assignments for parents to examine, and the teacher was available to answer any questions parents had about individual projects, tests, examinations, papers, and other assignments. Parents had a good grasp of what was expected of their children and how well they were living up to those expectations.

The purpose of the bimonthly community meetings was different. They were intended not so much to inform as to entertain parents, to provide an opportunity for the members of the community to socialize. Although I never had a chance to repeat my "valedictory address," I did recite Lincoln's Gettysburg Address. I had given it several times previously and so had thoroughly memorized it and didn't have to be prompted. As I declaimed, I glanced occasionally at my former teacher, Miss Scott; and every time our eyes met, she smiled and nodded at me. When I had finished and the polite applause subsided, Miss Scott rose to say she doubted that "there has been a better rendering of that address since Lincoln gave it himself." I didn't know whether I had been complimented or not; "rendering" was something the husband of our family cook did to a washpot full of fat pork with a huge fire crackling around it in the process of making lard. At that time, I hadn't then read the essay written by one of my graduate school professors, who argued that "the best statement of what the Civil War was *not* about is Lincoln's 'Gettysburg Address'"; so I proclaimed the words of that oration with the respect and awe I would have given, say, the Twenty-Third Psalm.

After each community meeting, the food (each family brought a "covered dish") was spread on a long table set up in the hall connecting the high school and grammar school. Then, for an hour or so, everyone ate and visited. Although nearly everyone went back for seconds and thirds, the amount of food on the table seemed to be unaffected. Long after everyone had eaten, parents and teachers stood about in small groups getting acquainted and rehashing details of community gossip.

One of the biggest events of the seniors' year was the senior play. Our class put on "Listen to Leon," a farce by Janice Gard. I suspect the primary reason it was selected was that it required only eight characters. Everyone in the senior class had a part, and only two had to be drafted from another class. Nearly fifty years later, I remember little about the play except that, for some reason, I was given the leading role.

There were some funny lines and episodes in the play, as Leon tried (by lying) to extricate himself from one compromising situation after another; but at the same time there were incidents associated with the play that I remember vividly. For example, one of the characters had a name whose pronunciation the cast could not agree on. The character Guiseppe was called everything from "Joe-SEEP" to "GUSE-pay. Another character spoke a line which the girl playing her could never learn to present. On the night of the production, she walked to the window and exclaimed: "My, my, who could that be? Coming up my drive?"—as if the latter question answered the former.

One good thing came out of the play, however: I had my first steady girlfriend. I took her home from each practice and saw her twice on weekends, for the movies on Saturday night and church on Sunday. I escorted her to the senior banquet, to the faculty party, to the cast party, and to several parties given by parents of seniors. I knew (or thought I knew) I was deeply in love, seeing her several times each week during the summer after graduation; but in the fall I went away to college, and she found another dear one from the local CCC camp.

Each member of the senior class received a little booklet entitled "Highlights of My Senior Year." In it, of course, members of the class were listed, along with the sponsor (the English teacher), the class officers, and the valedictorian and salutatorian. There was a place for the class colors, class flower, and class motto. The president of the class called a special meeting for the class to make a decision about these important matters. We quickly agreed (why, I no longer remember) on the class colors: black, white, and green, and the choice of class flower took almost no time. My suggestion of the rose was unanimously accepted. The class motto took considerably longer. No one apparently, could think of anything of sufficient dignity and challenge. After discarding several suggestions, the class poet suggested: "Not at the top but climbing."

Just before graduation (at which I was to give the salutatorian's address), I went to my teachers and classmates and asked them to write in my "memory booklet." One of my classmates wrote: "Here's wishing you much joy *thoughout* your *entire* life" (I didn't show that one to my English teacher). The class poet wrote: "Wishing you the greatest success along the trail of human life" (I didn't show that to anyone). My English teacher quoted the biblical verse beginning, "To thine own self be true. . . ." My coach wrote, very much in keeping with his philosophy, "Progress is made by work alone"; and my history teacher, who was also a Baptist minister, wrote: "Tonight, you launch out upon life's sea, hoping to reach the harbor in safety. Sail on, oh, gallant ship."

At the reception for the senior class given at the principal's house on Sunday afternoon following graduation, all the seniors—dressed in their best—greeted family, friends, and well-wishers. I wore my new suit, a graduation present from my father and mother.

After the festivities, Barkstol caught a ride back to our house. Everyone was sitting on the screened porch, eating homemade ice cream when he cleared his throat. "All you boys was so dressed up this evenin', I was reminded of a happnin' while I was workin' at Sumpter's Camp [a large sawmill]. One pay day a nigra got all dolled up and went stylin by where a high yeller was settin' on her front stoop. He styled by and said, 'Hey dar.'

"Hey dar," she said back to him.

He walked to the end of the block and styled back by, saying, "Hey dar."

He went up a few feet, turned and styled back by. "I say, is yo husban' to home?"

"Yeah," she said, "He in dar."

"Tell him," the dandy replied, "I say 'hey dar!'"

"That's not true," my mother said. "You know, Barkstol, you made every word of that up."

"'Tis, too," Barkstol responded. "I hope ever' hair on my head turns to a rattlesnake if it ain't."

Everyone was laughing too hard to notice whether Barkstol's hair had changed.

CHAPTER

6

What Do You Plan to Do?

College was a revelation. In my first class in sociology, I learned from a study conducted by Howard Odum and Estil Moore, two highly respected sociologists at the University of North Carolina, that the "plane of living" in Mississippi was about the lowest in the country. These social scientists based their conclusions on several measures of economic well-being: per capita income was the lowest in the forty-eight states, under $250 per year; less than twenty percent of the state's population was urban; the state had the fewest residential telephones; its inhabitants owned fewer radios and automobiles; they had less indoor plumbing and electricity and spent less money for public education, libraries, and museums than did any other state in the Union.

In one of his famous fireside chats, President Roosevelt labeled the South "the nation's number one economic problem." One evening on the radio, a well-known United States senator from Arkansas exclaimed, "Thank God for Mississippi. Only the presence of the Magnolia State keeps my state from being at the bottom of almost every statistical table printed in America." And a publisher in New York said on his radio show that there must be a very unusual educational system operating in Mississippi, one that taught everyone to write and no one to read. Each year, he said, he received more manuscripts for novels from Mississippi than he sold books in the state. A famous novelist wrote in the *Saturday Evening Post* that after long and sincere consideration, he had decided that "Mississippi is the state the nation can best afford to do without." A writer in the *Saturday Review of Literature* labeled Mississippi the state of the "Three B's: Bilboism, Bigotry and Backwardness." A reviewer in *The New Yorker,* writing about Faulkner's *Absalom, Absalom!,* pronounced: "There's nothing wrong with this novel except that it was written by a crazy man, and no one but a crazy man can understand it." Oscar Cargil's review in the *New York Times* wasn't much more favorable. Cargil concluded a brief essay, in which he accused Faulkner of being unable to write an intelligible sentence, by exclaiming: "This book is dull, dull, dull, dull, dull!"

Mississippi was widely regarded as possessing the most imperfect social order in the United States. Few supposedly civilized people had combined so obvious a sense of racial superiority with such a blatant system of social *in*justice. No more ignorant or more biased people had been given the franchise; after every election, the voters placed in high political office some of the country's most corrupt political demagogues. Even the powerful creative imagination of Robert Penn Warren found it difficult to imagine a social order with lower ethical standards. His fictional Willie Stark paled by comparison with Vardaman and Bilbo. In short, one would have expected a literary revival to occur in California, New York or Wisconsin, not in Mississippi. In an essay read before the Southern Literary Festival, Donald Davidson, summarizing the Odum–Moore study, observed: "Between 1925 and 1935 I don't see how Faulkner was able to stay alive in Mississippi, much less write."

Surprisingly, neither then nor later did I feel deprived; nor did I feel more depraved than most men. True, I had so often listened to the doctrine of man's imperfect state that I was convinced the doctrine was a valid description of man's condition. At the same time, I felt genuine affection for my family and a deep attachment to the place where I had been born and raised. I realized my family had little money to spare; but neither did anyone else. I was someone who belonged to a specific community. Living as I did within walking distance of the homes of seven aunts and uncles, where I passed much of my time, made me feel that family ties went beyond my own household. There was, too, the sense of belonging to a community composed of individuals, of school, church, and other institutions, which gave me a sense of belonging, of being a part of a particular place. Although I could not adequately put this feeling in words until much later in my life, I came to believe that, while the "plane of living" may have been low in the society in which I grew up, that society's "quality of life" was high.

When I went to college, I intended to follow in my father's footsteps and become a medical doctor. From the time I began high school, I had assisted my father in the office and accompanied him on house calls, even when the nature of the visit was so personal that I had to stay in the car. Once I got so cold waiting in the car that I went up and stood in the chimney corner to keep warm. From there I looked through a window and saw the birth of a child. To a sixteen-year-old, it was an informative and astounding, if not pleasant, sight. On more than one occasion, my father and I became stuck in a mud hole, and I had to walk a mile or more, wake a farmer, tell him our problem, go with him to the barn to catch and harness the mules, hook them to the wagon, and ride back to the car. When we hooked a chain from the wagon to the car, the farmer would yell at his mules and occasionally pop them with the end of the leather lines with which he steered them. Meanwhile, my father put the car in first gear and raced the motor. As soon as its wheels hit firm dirt, he would lift his foot from the accelerator and together he and the farmer would bring the car out of the hole. Once he failed to release the accelerator soon enough, and the car jumped forward and jammed the coupling pole of the wagon through the car's radiator. Regardless of the vehemence with which my father addressed God, nature, fate, and luck, his new car was considerably damaged.

With years of these kinds of experiences, I came to feel a deep affection for my father. When I went to college, therefore, I was determined to join him in the practice of medicine and enrolled in the premed program. At that time, a premed student was expected to prepare for the study of medicine by majoring in chemistry or biology, minoring in the subject in which he did not major. To support a major or gain the necessary skills that would be needed to practice medicine, the aspirant took two years of Latin, one of physics, and courses in mathematics, including calculus.

During my first year, I struggled through a rigorous program of mathematics and science, trying hard to assimilate the subject matter and accumulate the grades that would allow me to enter medical school. One day in the second semester of my sophomore year, I was sitting in calculus class when I suddenly realized that I did not know—and had not known for some time—what my professor was talking about. I seriously began to wonder if I were in the wrong field. As the semester progressed, my doubts grew. I began to consider changing my career objective.

What kept me from reaching a conclusion was fear of my father's reaction. I was afraid, quite naturally, that he would be terribly disappointed. Surely, the only reason I did not fail calculus was that during the review session at the end of the term my professor had given the class twenty-five "propositions" which, he said, would be similar to the questions on the examination. I had no alternative. The only way I could possibly prepare for the examination was to memorize the material the professor had given the class during the review sessions.

Although I spent all the time I could spare from preparing for my other examinations, even to the point of sitting up all night just before the exam, I could memorize only half the material given the class. I was so surprised when I looked at the copy of the examination the next day that I could scarcely breathe. I could hardly wait to begin writing. Four of the five questions I had memorized, and I knew them letter by letter. I wasn't going to fail the examination; I was going to make a B! In about twenty minutes, I carefully wrote from memory the ones I knew, then spent the remainder of the three-hour examination period trying to write something not completely stupid about the remaining question. Instead of realizing how fortunate I had been, I left the examination with a deep feeling of accomplishment; I had been rewarded for the long hours of work I had devoted to studying calculus—for what I hoped would be the last time in my life. As soon as I reached my dormitory room, the need for sleep caught up with me. I hadn't been to sleep for almost thirty hours, and I fell into bed and slept for twelve hours. When I went to collect my paper two days later, I found I had not a B but an A. Written across the top of the inside page was the note: "You spent so much time trying to do the first four questions perfectly that you did not leave sufficient time for the fifth." (I had done the first four in twenty minutes and struggled with the fifth for two hours and forty minutes.)

Before the next semester began, I had a few days at home. While there, I was determined to tell my father of my decision to change my major. In spite of my best efforts, however, I could not muster the courage to tell him what I was sure would be devastating news. Then too, there never seemed an appropriate occasion. One day, I rode with him on a professional call to a neighbor's, and on impulse blurted out: "I'm not smart enough to be a doctor. I've got to be something else." My father didn't seem nearly as shaken by this news as I had expected.

"I guess it's harder now than it was in my time," he said. "We didn't know much about medicine then. As you are aware, when I was graduated, one had to know little medicine: set a broken limb, deliver a baby, administer calomel and quinine." He paused, then asked: "What do you plan to do?"

It was my turn to be surprised. At first, I couldn't find my voice. "I don't know," I finally said. "I've just started to think about it."

When I returned, I withdrew from the premed program and without much thought given to what I would major in, continued the French course I was in and enrolled in two literature courses and two philosophy courses. From that time point on, college became a different experience. I began to enjoy it. Since I had completed all of the distribution requirements, (general courses required of all students, regardless of the area in which they wished to major), I continued for two or three semesters to take the courses I enjoyed and the ones in which I could do well without a great deal of effort.

One of my favorite courses was the English Romantic poets. The first topic explored in that course was, exactly what was the relationship between William and Dorothy Wordsworth? Why did the poet refer so often to "my sister" as my "dear, dear friend" and seldom mention his wife? Surely something beyond normal brother-sister affection was involved. Then we turned to Shelley and speculated on his attitude toward his wife Harriet. Surely his behavior was erratic and abnormal. Why was he so unkind to her? Was his treatment of her responsible for her suicide? The severity of his torturous behavior suggested to the instructor that Shelley might have been a sadist or even a masochist (two brand-new words in my vocabulary).

Then we came to a question that many times sent us to the library in search of an answer. *Precisely* what was the color of Keats' hair? One authority the class consulted wrote that his hair was auburn. Another indicated that it was sandy, with a tinge of red. Yet another claimed it was fiery red. What made the matter all the more perplexing was that all three of the sources had seen the poet while he was alive. How could they have had such widely varying reactions to something they had seen with their own eyes? The class was stumped. We were at a loss how to find the answer. Then the instructor said he would introduce us to *scholarship* and assigned one of the students a report on the work of a modern Keats scholar. As the student reported on the work of this scholar, it seemed that the answer was both simple and plausible: What had caused these three eyewitnesses to have different views of the color of Keats' hair was the simple fact that they had seen him in different kinds of light. In twenty-five pages of closely argued prose, the scholar demonstrated the validity of his thesis. He showed that one witness had seen Keats in bright sunlight and perceived his hair as red; another had seen him in the late afternoon and thus believed the poet's hair was "sandy, almost reddish." The third saw him one night at Leigh Hunt's under dim, artificial light and thus thought the poet's hair auburn. It now occurred to me that, with a little imagination and a lot of hard work, much could be accomplished.

Finally, the class came to Byron. We soon saw that much could be learned about this poet, some of it mind-boggling. What was the nature of his physical infirmity? Everyone agreed, it seemed, that he limped; but there was a division as to whether the limp was in his right foot or his left. The big question, though, and one on which the experts seemed about evenly divided, was: Did he, or did he not, have a clubfoot? That matter was so tangled and technical (just what is a clubfoot?) that the class finally decided that only a medical doctor would have enough knowledge of the right kind to follow the technical arguments; therefore, it was concluded that we could never be certain about the exact nature of Byron's deformity. We did not linger on our defeat long, however. We learned that despite his physical infirmity, Byron was a handsome devil (a kind of James Dean, Elvis Presley, or Boy George of his time) and that he had illegitimate children scattered across Europe. It was even hinted—though no one dared look up when the subject was discussed—that he might even have had an incestuous relationship with his own half-sister.

Now, all of this was most interesting (some of it was astounding) to a youth of nineteen born and raised in rural Mississippi, who, on a clear morning, could have seen the boundary of Yoknapatawpha County but had never heard of William Faulkner. We did everything but read and try to understand the poetry. The instructor read to us and had us memorize five hundred lines each week. I decided then and there that I was going to major in English; but I did not discover until ten years later, in a course in a different institution taught by one of the "New Critics," that some of these strange and unusual people had also written some pretty good poetry, that, though Byron lived by far the more interesting life, Keats was probably the better poet.

I went home for the summer before my senior year. One night, as I was pulling into our yard after having been out on a date, I heard a shotgun blast that seemed to come from the house across the road. As I looked in that direction, trying to determine the source of the blast, all the lights in the house suddenly came on. I rushed across the road, and the first thing I saw was the body of a boy with whom I had gone to high school. A few inches from his left hand (he was left-handed) was what looked like a .45 automatic (he had just been released from the army). On the front steps stood the fourteen-year-old son of my neighbor, a widow whose daughter the man on the ground had married a few months earlier and from whom he had been separated for a few weeks. Without asking what had happened, I ran back across the road, told my father, who had been awakened by the shot, what I had seen. He quickly dressed, grabbed his medical bag, and we rushed back across the road. He examined the boy and pronounced him dead, then told me to drive into town and tell the sheriff. The boy holding the gun said he would go in with me to give himself up. We found the sheriff at home, and the boy told him what had happened. The sheriff took him around to the jail, turned him over to the jailer, and followed me back to where the body lay.

My father was still there. The sheriff asked if the man was dead, and when my father said he was, telephoned for a hearse. Then he began trying to determine what had happened. He asked the widow, who said her daughter, the wife of the dead man, and her sister and brother had earlier that evening gone to a meeting at a nearby Holiness church. When the daughter was preparing to leave, her estranged husband, who appeared to be drunk, came up and said he wanted to talk to her. The daughter told him they had nothing to talk about, then got into the wagon and told her brother to drive home. The man followed the wagon the three miles home, cursing her and insisting that she talk to him. When the wife, her sisters, and brother got to the house, they jumped from the wagon and ran in. The estranged husband, the widow said, cursed her daughter, threatened her, pulled out his gun, and started toward the door. It was then that Hurley, the fourteen-year-old boy, walked to the door and shot him. Although I was sure I had seen a gun lying by the man's hand when I first saw him face down in the yard, the sheriff searched the premises thoroughly and could find no trace of the .45. (A small crowd, including the dead man's father and half-sister, had gathered at the scene while I went to get my father.)

The boy's friends and neighbors came to his support. He was charged with manslaughter, not murder. Then, two or three men went about the neighborhood collecting cash or anything that could be converted into cash until they had raised enough money to employ Marion W. Riley, one of the best criminal lawyers in the state, to defend the boy. When this development became known, excitement swept through the community. Hurley Cole's trial became the big event of the summer because the state was represented by a brilliant and aggressive young district attorney, who later became governor before being appointed a federal court judge.

It took three days to choose the jury. It had been a slow, tedious process because Riley was convinced, he said, that most criminal cases were won or lost in jury selection. Three or four witnesses were called by the district attorney: my father, who had pronounced him dead; the sheriff, to whom Hurley had admitted that he had killed the man; and I, who had observed some of events that night. Then the case went to the defense.

Marion Riley called character witnesses who testified that Hurley was a good boy who worked hard trying to help his widowed mother (actually, she earned a living for her family by taking in boarders), that the man who was killed was a heavy-drinking bully who spent many of his Saturday nights in jail for fighting, creating a public disturbance, and public drunkenness. Then Riley called me to the stand and asked in detail what I, the first outsider on the scene, had observed. He asked if I was sure it was a gun, and I assured him I was. Then Riley turned the case back to the prosecution, and the state's attorney called the sheriff back to the stand, along with others who had been there the night of the shooting. The questioning continued so long that I was exhausted. I reached the point where I hardly knew what I was saying. Finally, the district attorney dismissed me. Except for the summations to the jury, the trial was over. The district attorney was brief:

> A human being has been killed. The jury is to disregard the victim's unsavory reputation. The person who shot him has admitted his guilt. The only shred of evidence to support the possibility that the crime might have been provoked is the forty-five automatic, and only *one* witness saw, or thought he saw, that weapon. Although the defendant is a minor, he is being tried as an adult, and he is clearly guilty. Ladies and gentlemen of the jury, just do your duty and return a verdict of guilty of manslaughter as charged.

Riley's summation was lengthy and emotional. He presented in vivid detail a picture of a drunken, raging man whose past record clearly demonstrated that he was capable of murder. Riley loosened his tie and tears began to roll down his cheeks as he considered the plight of this fatherless boy who had to protect his defenseless mother and sisters. "Ladies and gentlemen, I am sure you will agree with me that day after day and sleepless night after sleepless night, he will receive far more punishment than he deserves. He really should be rewarded for having the courage to do what any son and brother could clearly see was his only choice. He had to pull that trigger, whether he wanted to or not."

The jury deliberated less than ten minutes before returning a verdict of not guilty.

Downtown Louisville, 1920s

Will and Lula Young with their first child on the porch of their new home soon after it was built in 1906. They lived here until Will died in 1962.

Will and Lula Young, 1950

The author, waiting for D-Day, Martlesham Heath near Ipswich

Richmond Croom Beatty, late 1940s

Dan Young, 1941

Donald Davidson, late 1940s

Walter Clyde Curry, late 1940s

Dan Young speaking at a memorial service for John Crowe Ransom, Kenyon College, 1975

Dan and Arlease Young, 1984

CHAPTER

7

Look at this Program and Tell Me What You Think of It

When I returned to college in the fall, I followed my parents' advice and enrolled in the education courses required to obtain a certificate to teach in high school. I agreed with them: there were few ways to earn a living with a major in English. After I had enrolled in the education courses and the practice teaching—especially since I was assigned to practice teach in a village ten miles from the college—there was no time during the fall term for any other courses except one in French, which I arranged to take on Saturday mornings in the instructor's home. (There were no regularly scheduled classes on Saturday.) I was eager to get this course in French because if I did not have the first term of the course, I could get nothing in the field during the second term and thus would not be able to complete my double major in English and French.

The next semester, I continued the French and enrolled in two English courses and two philosophy courses. In early February, however, the draft board notified me that I was to report two months hence for a physical examination. Although the United States had not entered the war in Europe, nearly everyone was convinced it was only a matter of time before it would. I was depressed. I was convinced that I would be drafted as soon as I graduated, which would not be until the end of the summer session because of my change of major. When I reported for my physical examination, however, I was rated 4F because of a chronic inflammation of my inner ear. This meant I was exempt from military service and returned to school. In late April, I accepted a position teaching English at a nearby high school.

In early June, on the first day of registration, I was assisting in the registrar's office when I noticed Arlease Lewis at the end of a long line. I had been in school with her during the first two years, but we had transferred to different schools at the beginning of our junior year. As soon as I had finished registering the student with whom I was working, I went over to where she stood and asked how she came to be there. Hadn't she graduated?

"Yes," she replied; "I graduated. I came here to get some library science courses required by the State Department of Education for certification to teach high school English. Why are you here?"

"I came to get some professional courses in teaching, so I can be certified in the same field." I then slipped her past a long line of students and into the office where registration was being held. When we had finished, I suggested that we go to the movies and catch up on others news. In the school we had previously attended, we knew each other well. Although we ate at the same table in the dining hall, we had never been out together. She agreed, and I promised to call for her at the dormitory at seven.

The afternoon dragged by, and at seven o'clock, I called for her. We went to the movies and stopped on our way back to the campus for a Coke and something to eat. I asked if she were free the following evening.

After that, we saw each other every day and almost every evening. I had had the courses Arlease was taking and, as the librarian's assistant, had to teach them when she had something else to do, which was at least half of the time. I was able to help her study for the tests and examinations, reading her papers and in general teaching her.

The more I saw of Arlease, the better I liked her. I fell in love and asked her to marry me. She invited me to her home in Rose Hill to meet her parents. I went on a Saturday afternoon and talked with her father (her mother was in Washington), spending the night with a cousin of hers who lived nearby. The next day, I returned to Hattiesburg. When I saw Arlease on Monday evening, I asked if she had reached a decision. She had, and we decided to marry the following year, after we had completed our contracts for the next school year.

The school at which I taught the following year was much like that from which I had been graduated five years earlier. I was assigned all the English classes from the seventh through the twelfth grades with fifteen to twenty-five students in each class. Since the eleventh and twelfth grades were combined, I had a few more than a hundred students spread over five classes. I spent my two free periods keeping study hall or working in the library.

Living conditions at the school were unique in my experience. Five bachelors lived in the home furnished by the school for the superintendent. Since the home was unfurnished, we went to Sears and bought a stove, refrigerator, a dining table and six chairs, and a living-room suite. (Two of the teachers lived nearby and brought bedroom furniture and linens from home; the others had to buy theirs.) One of the young men brought a cow from home, which he milked; and we employed a cook for five dollars a week, who prepared us two meals a day. (The other we ate in the lunch room.) We elected one of the teachers, a business major, financial manager, and he made the installment payments on the furniture, paid the cook and the utilities bill, then he divided the total by five. Each of us never had to pay more than eight dollars a month, a fact in which I rejoiced, since I was only making eighty-five.

The greatest problem I faced was boredom. Since we didn't have a car, we had little to do—except when the superintendent would occasionally let us accompany him to an all-day singing—but read, talk to each other, and listen to the radio. In the first two or three weekends, we exhausted these possibilities.

On the afternoon of December 7, 1941, I was listening to the radio with one of the other teachers when I heard that the Japanese had bombed Pearl Harbor. A declaration of war would surely follow, and I might be called into service despite my 4F classification. Arlease and I conferred by telephone that evening, and decided to move our wedding date up to December 21, despite the likelihood of my having to go into service. We married as planned, though we couldn't live together because both of us had to complete teaching contracts in schools approximately a hundred miles apart. Until school was out, we would have to see each other only on weekends.

As soon as school was out, in late May, I got my affairs in order. I knew the call for another physical examination would come at any time. On June 5, 1942, I was requested to report to Camp Shelby a week hence. Although I still had the ear inflammation, I was convinced I wouldn't be exempted again. Therefore, Arlease, my bride of four months, and I made plans for her to join me as soon as I finished basic training and was assigned to a permanent station.

When I reported to Camp Shelby, I met a friend from college. He, too, was awaiting induction. The next morning at daylight, a corporal stuck his head in the tent and yelled: "Fall in!" My group of eight joined about a hundred others and were marched to breakfast, after which we were again assembled and marched to the examining station. As we awaited our turn to see the doctors, a noncommissioned officer came down the line asking if anyone in the line could use a typewriter. Having already been warned to volunteer for nothing, I remained silent. My friend, however, admitted that he could "type a little," whereupon he was pulled from the line and marched away. When I reached the appropriate station, he was seated behind a typewriter and completed my induction papers. Nearly four years later, also at Camp Shelby, the same man completed my discharge papers. He had remained at the induction center throughout the war.

I hardly stopped again. No one even looked in my ears. Fifteen minutes later, I was in another tent, this one much like the one I had left an hour earlier, hastening to change into an ill-fitting uniform. I was to be fully dressed and in front of company headquarters in "ten damn minutes," and I didn't feel like doing a "hunderd" laps for being one minute late.

From Shelby I went to Keesler Field, thence to the Hotel Stevens in Chicago for instructions in radio operation and maintenance and from there to Boca Raton, Florida, for instruction in some strange new field no one even mentioned the name of. We later learned that we were to be instructed in a top-secret device called radar. Upon completion of this training, I was sent to Westover Field, in Massachusetts, to join a combat outfit. I received combat training in New York, Connecticut (where Arlease joined me), and New Hampshire before being shipped overseas, on September 5, 1943, to join the Eighth Air Force in England.

After serving briefly as communications officer with a fighter squadron, I was assigned as commander of a squad of twelve men manning a radar unit near Land's End, in the south of England. I was allowed to select the men for this assignment from a pool in a fighter group. All of those I chose had strong backgrounds in the humanities and a lively interest in modern literature. Of the thirteen, including me, seven later received the Ph.D., two became lawyers, two stockbrokers, one a successful playwright, and one the fiction editor of a magazine of national circulation.

It soon became apparent that we would have a great deal of spare time; in the year we were there, we received only one call, and that to test our equipment. We were there to spot Hitler's V-1 "buzz bombs," which were being launched over the north of England toward London. These would be tracked by radar stations in Bury St. Edmonds and Nottingham. To avoid boredom we devised a plan to occupy our time. Since only four men were needed to work each of the three eight-hour shifts per day, there was always an extra man. That man was available for a journey to London—everyone had his turn (in alphabetical order) fulfilling this duty—where he acquired copies of all the books available, both new and second-hand, of the author we currently happened to be interested in. When he returned, the books were passed around and read, after which there would be animated discussions of plot, technique, meaning, strengths and weaknesses, and other points of interest. These discussions would send the readers back to reread parts of books, and sometimes entire books, to see if they could understand why a particular person had read a certain book as he had. Often, these discussions required reading aloud specific portions of a book, particular passages of poetry, to illustrate how one had arrived at the reading he had or how he had reached a particular conclusion. In this manner, I read—really read—T. S. Eliot, Ezra Pound, James Joyce, Marcel Proust, Aldous Huxley, Edith Sitwell, Virginia Wolfe, Katherine Mansfield, and John Millington Synge. I later wondered why there were so few American writers among those I had studied and, specifically, why William Faulkner had not been mentioned.

This pleasant (and very profitable episode) in my life ended abruptly when it was finally determined that Hitler wasn't going to send any of his buzz bombs over the southern route. With the Allies beginning to think seriously about the invasion of Europe—what was already beginning to be referred to in secret communications as D-Day—my group was sent back to Eighth Air Force headquarters for reassignment. I was assigned as a radio operator on a C-47. After days of seemingly endless practice at a base near London, carrying a load of paratroopers inside the plane and tugging a glider filled with troops behind, the long-awaited day arrived. In one day alone, my crew made six trips across the English Channel. Then the demands for our services became fewer and fewer and finally ceased altogether. I returned to Eighth Air Force headquarters.

In the spring of 1945, like several million other Americans, I was in England with absolutely nothing to do. VE Day had come; the enemy in Europe was finally defeated; and for the first time since leaving Land's End, I found myself trying hard to find some constructive way to spend my time. Suddenly, displaying a wisdom seldom shown by that organization, the military began to devise schemes to occupy the idle time of those who saw no reason for remaining in Europe now that their mission had been accomplished, but who could not yet go home. First, a G.I. University was established in England so those who had joined the service directly out of high school could go to college. This program met none of my needs, however, although I did briefly consider applying to join its faculty. I had already completed my degree and taught for a year.

Just when I had about decided that, despite a surplus of combat points (a fact that should ensure my rotation back to the States), I was going to have to remain idle in Europe, I was called into Lieutenant Morrisey's office. Handing me a long, mimeographed sheet, Morrisey said: "Look at this program and tell me what you think of it." I could hardly believe what I read. It was an invitation for twenty G.I.s with undergraduate majors in English to spend six weeks at Oxford listening to Professor J. Dover Wilson, a leading authority in the field, lecture on Shakespeare. After the lectures, the group would go to Stratford-upon-Avon and London to see the plays on which Wilson had lectured. Furthermore, at Stratford, the students would hear lectures from members of the cast and would be able to go backstage to learn first-hand how a professional group produced a drama.

As I stood there, still unable to speak, Lieutenant Morrisey said,

"If you want to go, I'll put your name on the list. If you know of anyone else who's qualified, we'll add his name." Immediately I thought of five of the group who had been with me at Land's End who had degrees in English and who were right there in the headquarters squadron. I wrote my name and theirs at the bottom of the announcement and headed back to the reading room of the Red Cross canteen, where I had left the others a few minutes before.

Three weeks later, my five friends, fourteen other American servicemen, and I met Professor Wilson, his wife, and daughter in the dining room of an Oxford College for a reception, the first organized activity of the lecture series. The first lecture, on *Hamlet,* was scheduled for nine o'clock the following day. My friends and I had read the play more than once and had discussed it for the past two weeks. The next morning, we were the first ones in the lounge where the lectures were to be held. Remaining seated, Professor Wilson began speaking in an informal tone, first giving some critical opinions of the play, as well as his own assessment of these opinions. He presented some interpretations given Hamlet by some of the great Shakespearean actors who had played the the leading role in the play, then concluded with his own reading of the drama. Some members of the class learned later that what Professor Wilson had said was essentially what he had written about the play in his book, *What Happens in "Hamlet."* The greatest surprise of the morning, other than the fact that no one could believe that Professor Wilson had talked for three hours (with a short break for tea)— was that, after his introductory remarks, he had *discussed* the play. We were unaccustomed to such teaching. Like this one, many of Wilson's other lectures on Shakespeare's dramas were based on another of his books, *The Essential Shakespeare*.

After the lectures, we went to Stratford and registered at the Washington Irving Hotel, where we stayed until we had seen, at the Shakespeare Theatre, performances of the plays we had studied. We had pretty much a free run of the theater. Those who wished could sit in the audience and observe the play from there; others could go backstage and view the nuts and bolts of a major theater operation—visit the dressing rooms of the players, observe the application of make-up, watch the stage directors as they gave entrance and exit cues or prompted an actor or actress who missed a line. I was amazed at the complex system of lighting—the many times when the lights on the stage were lowered or brightened, how the speaker usually received an almost imperceptible increase of light, just enough to direct the attention of the members of the audience without their realizing it. I was also amazed at the size of the staff and the efficiency with which they performed their duties.

On the morning following a production, Professor Wilson would invite a member of the cast or someone from the production or director's staff to talk to us. Invariably, the actors and actresses talked about their perception of the dramatic function of the character they were portraying and about the techniques they were employing in attempting to make audiences aware of the character's function. One of the most impressive such presentations was that of the actress who played the nurse in *Romeo and Juliet*. She took about an hour to explain the character's role in the drama, although that character has only a half dozen or so lines. The director or the director's assistant concentrated on what he believed to be Shakespeare's intentions in the play and how he was attempting to accomplish the playwright's objectives. The other members of the staff explained their specific professional responsibilities. Usually after these presentations there was about an hour for tea and conversation between us and the representatives of the cast.

When we had seen all the plays that were being presented at Stratford, everyone, including the Wilsons, went to London to see Ralph Richardson and Laurence Olivier in *Henry IV*, parts 1 and 2, John Gielgud in *Hamlet*, and Donald Wolfit in *King Lear*. After each performance, Professor Wilson gave a complete evaluation of it. The entire experience surpassed anything any of us had ever participated in.

Each day of the nearly three years I was in England, I wrote Arlease, explaining in detail the experiences I was having. She, in turn, wrote me daily, giving me the details of her teaching in high school. For both of us, the time seemed endless. I sometimes wondered whether we would ever be together again. Too, there were weekly letters from my mother and sisters, keeping me informed of family news and telling me I was missed. I learned that Myrta's husband Lamar was stationed near me, a member of a B-24 group, and one weekend, I went to see him. When I arrived, he was on a mission, so I waited. When his plane returned about two hours later, I was waiting on the flight line. I could tell before he landed that his plane had had a rough mission; only two of its four engines were operating. Then I heard two ambulances headed for the plane's parking slot. The thought went through my mind that Lamar had been wounded or killed. He was all right, though the ball-turret gunner was mutilated. For the first time, I began to understand Randall Jarrell's "Death of the Ball Turret Gunner." As I observed the bubble he occupied on the bomber's underside, completely exposed to enemy fighters, I understood why his position was considered one of the most dangerous in the Air Force.

While stationed in London, far removed from the action, I became acquainted with a group of poets who were publishing a small poetry magazine. Wrey Gardiner, the editor of the journal, was operating a tiny publishing firm called the Grey Wall Press, and he accepted four of my poems. Reading these poems in later years, I can well agree with those readers who have repeatedly told me that poetry is not my field.

CHAPTER
8

This Might Be Your Only Chance to Meet Faulkner

Two weeks after we returned to our outfit, the commanding officer was notified that the Office of Special Services was recruiting fifty men with two years of college-level French who wanted to spend an academic year studying French language and culture at the Sorbonne. Although signing up for the program would likely delay my going home for a few months, I immediately indicated my interest, as did three of my friends who had had the Shakespeare course. Since I had a major in French in college, I was placed in charge of the group to see that they made the trip safely from London to the Lycée Louis le Grande in Paris, which included the residence hall in which we would live during our year at the university.

One of my first discoveries was learning that the language I thought I could read and speak fairly well in the classroom of my American university had not made its way to Paris, and that I would have been intellectually isolated had not the French lectures been available in printed form before they were given, and had not my French friends spoken proper Oxfordian English.

My instructor in the small section of French language I took (only twelve in the class) insisted that everyone speak French all the time. If a student attempted to ask a classmate a question, the instructor would interrupt and say in French, "You are being impolite because I do not speak English." About the only time English was spoken was in the dormitory at night or with the French students at school. If a group of French students were conversing in French and an American walked up, they would immediately switch to English without missing a word. When I gained a little confidence, I would speak to them in French, and they would respond in English. My having to rely on French exclusively in class helped considerably; at the end of the course, I had not been paid for several months, and I needed some money for incidentals on the trip home. I sold some cigarettes, candy bars, and articles of clothing on the black market. The entire transaction was in French. The instructor who made the class converse in French because he didn't speak English conducted the last session in impeccable Oxfordian English, while insisting that the Americans speak French. I felt so sure of my French that, when I was thinking of graduate school, I couldn't decide whether to study English or French.

In addition to the course in French language and culture, I was able to enroll in a course in the modern novel. My most humiliating experience there involved a fellow Mississippian. As Jean-Paul Sartre was to tell Malcolm Cowley several years later, "After the war, Faulkner was regarded as a god by the French youth." Since I was both an American and a Mississippian, all of my French acquaintances assumed that I was an authority on Faulkner. Alas, the only Faulkner story I had read was "Barn Burning." I had, of course, heard of the infamous *Sanctuary* and had read two novels in French, *Pylon* and *The Hamlet*. One night at a party I was appalled to hear a young French girl summarize the plot of "A Rose for Emily" and hastened to inform her that Faulkner's story was not an accurate portrayal of the way the *good* people of Mississippi lived and behaved. I was deeply troubled and confused by discussions of a Snopses–Sartoris controversy because in the only story I had read, the principal character was named Colonel Sartoris Snopes. Why, I wondered, did one name a son for a mortal enemy? I later learned that there are many grades of morality among the Snopeses, that Sarty was the best of the lot, and that it was this fact Faulkner was attempting to convey in the name.

My term at the Sorbonne ended, and I booked passage home. Three days after sailing from Southhampton, I stood on the deck of the *Queen Elizabeth,* looking at the New York skyline. To me, it seemed unfamiliar. I'd shipped out from New York three years earlier, but I had never had a good view of New York from the sea. When I sailed from this port, it was in the hold of a troop ship, and I couldn't see anything. Then, too, this wasn't my section of the country. I had lived practically all of my life in Mississippi and now was excited at the thought of returning home and seeing my parents and other members of my family, especially my wife Arlease.

As eager as I was to get home, I allowed myself a few days in New York in order to collect some of the books of the man the French claimed was the equal of Hawthorne, Melville, or Henry James. In New York, I learned that the only Faulkner book in print was *Sanctuary* and that even that book wasn't available at any of the seven or eight bookstores at which I inquired. (By this time Faulkner had written seventeen books, including all of those on which his reputation is now based.) The card catalogue of the New York Public Library, which I visited on my second day in the city, carried the titles of two of Faulkner's works: *Soldier's Pay* and *The Hamlet.* An assistant in the library directed me to the second-hand bookstores on Fourth Avenue, where I secured first editions of *Go Down, Moses* and *Mosquitoes* for fifty cents each and a second-hand copy of the Modern Library edition of *Sanctuary* for twenty-five cents. I had to be content with these finds; nothing else was available. Soon after I arrived in Mississippi, an inquiry to Seven Bookhunters, a New York firm, brought an offer of a first edition of *Pylon* for the then exorbitant price of five dollars. I added this title to what might then have been the best Faulkner collection in Mississippi outside of Oxford.

At the appointed time, I reported to Fort Hamilton, where I was placed on the only bona fide troop train I saw during the war. It consisted of about a hundred box cars that had been converted into sleepers by installing eight double bunks and sixteen canvas chairs in each car. The train proceeded slowly. We were shunted onto a siding every time we met a passenger or freight train. In addition, we stopped each morning and twice during the afternoon to give the men a chance to answer the call of nature. We stopped for each meal, and the men took their mess gear and lined up beside one of the two cars that had become kitchens, where we were served small amounts of the worst food I have ever eaten any where at any time.

I had talked to Arlease by telephone from New York and knew she was taking a week off from school so we could have a second honeymoon. I finally arrived at Camp Shelby, where a friend who was processing my discharge papers told me he had spoken to Arlease, and she was waiting for me at her cousin's house in Hattiesburg. But since the train had taken five days from New York, we had only two days left. I finished all of the many details required of me and walked out the door. There I found a bus waiting to take discharged soldiers into town. Thinking I might miss the bus and have to wait an hour for another, I didn't even go to the barracks next door to get my barracks bags, but left everything I had collected in Europe (what I hadn't mailed home) and went into the station, where I was met by a friend who took me to Arlease. To my great delight, she had arranged to get off another week; so we had nine glorious days together. When our time was almost over, we spent a couple of days with my parents, then went to Rose Hill, where Arlease lived and taught.

I had hoped to enroll in graduate school but was surprised and dismayed to learn I couldn't be admitted until the summer session. Returning G.I.s were flooding the schools. But at the home of Arlease's parents, I met with good news. One of the woman teachers had resigned to go to California to be with her husband who had returned after three years, so there was a vacancy in Rose Hill High School. Hired to fill the position, I taught and coached and lived with Arlease's parents for the remainder of the school year.

In June 1946, I enrolled in graduate school at the University of Mississippi, and quickly thereafter a series of events occurred that were among the most exciting of my life. The first thing I did after arriving in Oxford was to try to find William Faulkner in the telephone directory; but no such person was listed. Disappointed, I convinced myself that such an important person would have an unlisted phone. Then I learned from an advertisement at the Lyric Theater, one of Oxford's two movie houses, that a man named William Falkner had two birddogs for sale and that anyone interested in purchasing one of these animals should call a number listed on the screen. While trying to get up the courage to pretend an interest in birddogs, I learned from a friend that Faulkner came to the post office about ten each morning, collected his mail, and retired to the Gathwright–Reed Drugstore to read the mail and share a cup of coffee with his friend, Mac Reed. My friend and I spent a great deal of time speculating on the contents of the parcels Faulkner occasionally carried to or brought from the post office (a new manuscript or proofs of one already in press?). We discovered, too, that most evenings, Faulkner could be found in the No Parking zone in front of the theater, sitting on the hood of his ten-year-old car, one with a homemade oil-cloth top, smoking his pipe, and waiting for his daughter, Jill, to come out of the movie.

During the 1947–48 session, while writing my master's thesis, I took a job as instructor of English and taught three sections of freshman English and one section of the survey of English literature. One of my students in the English survey course was Malcolm Franklin, Faulkner's stepson. One day Malcolm asked me to come to his house for a drink and meet "Pappy," his name for Faulkner. I hesitated. Malcolm was barely passing my course, and I thought he might be trying to score points and thus raise his grade. But I quickly made up my mind. *This might be your only chance to meet Faulkner,* I told myself, *so you had better grab it.* "OK," I said to Malcolm, "I'll see you at five."

About ten people were there when I arrived. Faulkner was playing host in the manner of a Southern gentleman. Introducing me, Malcolm told Faulkner I was from Louisville, and Faulkner asked if I knew several people who lived there. Of course, I did. After several minutes of polite conversation, Faulkner said he was taking drink orders and asked each of us what we would have. When my turn came I said, "I'll have bourbon and water." After Faulkner had asked everyone, he said: "I believe I'll have a toddy." Then I remembered his description of the toddy that Jupiter made Old Bayard every afternoon. "I believe I'll change my mind and have a toddy with you, Mr. Faulkner." When the drinks came, everyone had ice except Faulkner and me. I looked down at my glass and saw that it was one-third full of sugar, with a little bourbon, water, and twist of lemon on top. That was absolutely the worst drink I have ever had. I looked over at Faulkner, but he seemed to be enjoying his drink immensely.

My first-hand acquaintance with Faulkner took on added significance in the spring of 1946. In April of that year, Malcolm Cowley's *Portable Faulkner* appeared, and I began to perceive—though still indistinctly, since I had yet to read more than a half dozen of the novels, and those selected on the basis of availability—some of the reasons why Faulkner was causing such excitement in France. "There in Oxford," as Cowley points out in one the most influential introductions to the work of a literary figure to appear in this century, "Faulkner performed a labor of imagination that has not been equaled in our time, and a double labor: first, to invent a Mississippi county that was like a mythical kingdom . . . second, to make his story of Yoknapatawpha County stand as a parable or legend of all the Deep South." Cowley describes in some detail this mythical kingdom and what it symbolizes:

> Faulkner's mythical kingdom is a county in northern Mississippi, on the border between the sand hills covered with scrubby pine and the black earth of the river bottoms. Except for the storekeepers, mechanics, and professional men who live in Jefferson, the county seat, all the inhabitants are farmers or woodsmen. Except for a little lumber, their only product is baled cotton for the Memphis market. A few of them live in big plantation houses, the relics of another age, and more of them in substantial wooden farmhouses; but most of them are tenants, no better housed than slaves on good plantations before the Civil War. Yoknapatawpha County . . . has a population of 15,611 persons scattered over 2400 square miles.
>
> . . . . .
>
> Although the pattern is presented in terms of a single Mississippi county, it can be extended to the Deep South as a whole.
>
> . . . . .
>
> It can be found in the whole fictional framework that he has been elaborating in novel after novel, until his work has become a myth or legend of the South.

I read Cowley's introduction with great care and was able to see for the first time a unifying design in the novels and stories, a continuing thematic concern clearly demonstrated in the more than seven hundred pages of selections Cowley included in the book. The reaction to *The Portable Faulkner* exceeded its publisher's most optimistic expectations.

In a later book, Cowley described Faulkner's critical reputation in America when *The Portable Faulkner* was published. Although Faulkner was highly regarded by his fellow writers, the critics and publishers held a quite different view. "The bright boys among the critics," Cowley wrote Faulkner in 1944, "did a swell job of [not] comprehending and underselling you, Fadiman especially" (in a review of *Absalom, Absalom!* in the *New Yorker,* Fadiman had written: "There's nothing wrong with this book except it was written by a crazy man and no one but a crazy man could understand it.") The critics, Cowley concluded, had convinced the publishers that Faulkner's books would not sell, which meant that Cowley couldn't place the long essay that eventually became the introduction to *The Portable Faulkner.* To use a Mississippi expression, he "beefed" it (from the practice of selling steaks and roasts from a side of beef); that is, he cut the article up and published sections of it in the *New Republic,* the *New York Times Book Review,* and the *Sewanee Review,* in the last of which the excerpted essay won a prize as best essay of the year.

After these articles appeared (in rapid succession), one of the editors at Viking, the very publisher who had earlier turned down Cowley's request for a portable Faulkner, called Cowley. "I've noticed that Faulkner is receiving quite a bit of attention in the journals," he said. "Perhaps we'd better go ahead with your project."

So *The Portable Faulkner* was published. It was widely read and well received, but I felt that Cowley's helpful introduction was too restrictive. When I read Robert Penn Warren's review in the *New Republic,* I understood better what was troubling me about the introduction. Warren asserted that Cowley's essay is one of the few things written on Faulkner that is not "hag ridden by prejudice or preconception and which sheds some light on the subject." He expressed the emphatic belief that Cowley's introduction was the "most important essay every written on Faulkner," but at the same time he was worried about its major concerns. "It is important," he wrote,

> that Faulkner's work be regarded not in terms of the South against the North, but in terms of issues which are common to our modern world. The legend is not merely a legend of the South, but it is also a legend of our general plight and problem.

It reflects, Warren insisted, the moral confusion, the lack of discipline, the loss of a sense of mission by Western civilization. I was beginning to see a little more clearly the attraction of this Mississippi writer for those French students.

I read every review I could find and was impressed by most of them. The ones I found most informative were those that cited not only the great need for such a book as *The Portable Faulkner* and complimented highly the introductory essay but insisted that in his introduction Cowley does not emphasize sufficiently the mythopoeic quality of Faulkner's creative imagination. This quality, one these commentators believe (correctly, I think) is disappearing under the onslaught of modern science, is the only avenue left open to contemporary humanity to share common beliefs, the only way to become aware of things metaphysical. To these critics, the use of archetypes—communicable universal symbols through which people can transcend the bounds of positivistic materialism—is a significant aspect of Faulkner's work virtually ignored by Cowley. (Cowley has since stated publicly his agreement with the claims made by Warren and the other critics.) Much of the recent criticism of Faulkner follows one or the other of these suggestions; the only exceptions I found are the source-hunters, the intentionalists, and the Freudians.

Warren's statement that the Cowley essay/introduction is one of the few sensible critiques of Faulkner's work that has been published sent me back to the reviews to see what had already been published about the "writing man from Oxford." Although I found perceptive, informative studies by Arnold Bennett, Kay Boyle, Evelyn Scott, L. A. G. Strong, Conrad Aiken, and Jean-Paul Sartre, most American critics seemed unaware of Faulkner's creative intentions, as well as oblivious to his genius. Faulkner was called the chief exponent of the "cult of cruelty," a writer "obsessed with unpleasant subjects," one who was fond of "inventing his stories in a regular intelligible form and then distorting them." He was proclaimed "a salesman of vice," a writer who fills his novels with "monstrous beings." More than one critic found Faulkner's work markedly inferior to that of Erskine Caldwell. Oscar Cargill's evaluation of *Absalom, Absalom!* was almost as damning as that of Clifton Fadiman. Cargill labeled the novel "dull book, dull, dull, dull."

I came to the conclusion that, in general, Faulkner was accused of being a member of a dying class who "cling to their self-loving myths of the past, glorifying themselves with the gaudy legends of their ancestors until the sound of their names becomes to them like 'silver pennons downrushing at sunset.'" (The last phrase is quoted from *Intruder in the Dust*.)

With the publication of Cowley's *Portable Faulkner* and the essays of Warren and a few others, the critical-evaluation situation quickly and drastically changed. Close on the heels of Cowley's publication came the Modern Library's one-volume edition of *The Sound and the Fury* and *As I Lay Dying,* a volume that was soon added to the required-reading list of almost every modern American novel course in the country. Faulkner's novels began to come back into print, and Hollywood made a film of *Intruder in the Dust*. Harry M. Campbell (one of my professors, who, with Ruel Foster of the University of West Virginia, was co-authoring the first book-length study of Faulkner's fiction) appeared in a crowd scene.

When I became an instructor in the English department, I found that every short-story anthology sent me for adoption in my course contained at least one story by Faulkner. He was finally persuaded to come to the university to speak to some of the classes, one of them mine, and for the first time I heard him give his now famous list of the five most important modern American novelists, which included Wolfe, himself, and Hemingway, in that order. Faulkner later gave this list many times, and often changed the names and the order; but he always included Wolfe, Faulkner, and Hemingway. Although several commentators claim that the Nobel Prize committee had Faulkner's name under consideration before the publication of *The Portable Faulkner,* I felt then and now that the wave of recognition and praise Faulkner received after publication of *The Portable Faulkner* must have influenced at least some members of the committee.

The Nobel Prize, along with other prizes, awards, and honors, made Faulkner famous and his name familiar to those who had never read any of his books. At the same time, the availability of his books, as well as the attention given his stories and novels in schools and colleges, vastly increased his audience. The publication of Campbell and Foster's *William Faulkner: A Critical Appraisal* and Hoffman and Vicker's *Two Decades of Criticism*—not to mention the appearance of important critical articles by Lawrence Bowling, Richard Chase, George Marion O'Donnell, and others—enhanced Faulkner's reputation. I was convinced that never had the reputation of an American writer owed as much to the publication of a single book as Faulkner's had to Cowley's *Portable Faulkner.* Now that I had been able to read and study Faulkner's oeuvre, as well as much of the criticism, I wished I were back in France, among those whose admiration for the most famous citizen of my native state seemed to approach worship.

Faulkner could now earn a living by writing; there was no longer any need for extended stints in Hollywood. But as any student of Faulkner's work now knows, and as I soon learned, Faulkner's best work had been done. Not until *The Reivers,* published in 1962, would he again write at the level which had produced *The Sound and the Fury, As I Lay Dying, Light in August, Absalom, Absalom!, The Hamlet,* and *Go Down, Moses.* Numerous critics tried to account for this decline. Some suggested that he was no longer hungry enough, that there was too much money to be made from book sales, movie and television rights, and lecture appearances. Others, Donald Davidson among them, argued that Faulkner had begun to take his public image too seriously. He became a cultural ambassador to South America and Japan; he spoke at the Delta Council, to his daughter Jill's graduating classes at the University High School and the Pine Manor Junior College, to the Southern Historical Association, the U.S. National Commission for UNESCO. He wrote essays for *Holiday, Sports Illustrated, Harper's,* and *Life.*

Working on my Ph.D., I searched for an answer to the perplexing question of Faulkner's declining creative powers. Faulkner was still turning out fiction, much of it as carefully and painstakingly composed as the great novels of 1929 to 1942. In 1950, *The Fable* appeared. It was a novel Faulkner had long worked on, one which, he often suggested, might be his magnum opus. In 1957 appeared *The Town* and, in 1959, *The Mansion.* The latter he called "the final chapter of and the summation of a work conceived of in 1925." Cowley, in pointing out that the Snopes story was unfinished, called on Faulkner to finish it.

I read *Intruder in the Dust* and *The Town* as they appeared. Except for the Mink Snopes section of *The Mansion,* I could not share the enthusiasm with which they were received. Then, too, there seemed to be an uneasiness in some of the reviews. What was wrong? These were good books, but they lacked the imaginative daring of the earlier novels.

As I reread and thought about *A Fable,* its basic weakness became apparent. It wasn't, as I had first thought, that Faulkner had moved outside his little "postage stamp of earth" and was less familiar with his characters and new situations. What was wrong was that Faulkner was overly restricting the range and freedom of his imagination. The novel converts the archetypal Christian myth on which it is based into a rigid allegory; the author's attitude toward his material is more that of the rhetorician than the artist. Faulkner presents his fable with a doctrinal single-mindedness that permits no creative critical reading. He prescribes the expected response and sets definite limits on the range of perception allowed the reader. I decided then, and have not changed my mind since, that the failure of *A Fable* is the direct result of Faulkner's use of what Allen Tate has called the "rhetorical imagination," the mode used by social scientists and theologians, not the mode of the artist.

Trying to determine the imperfections of *The Town* and *The Mansion* was far more difficult. I was unable to articulate my reaction to these novels until after I had read Cleanth Brook's 1963 study, *William Faulkner: The Yoknapatawpha Country*. As Brooks points out, in *The Hamlet*, Flem and Eula are creatures that cannot be measured by the ordinary standards of this world:

> Eula is a woman of fabulous beauty and seductive power, though unself-conscious and almost unaware of that power. She becomes the archetypical female—at least in the eyes of the young fanatic Labove, and in a sense she becomes such for the entire community. And Flem, in his sheer concern for money and the power it brings, becomes something fabulous too.... [T]he impotent Flem, who is pure single-minded acquisitiveness, and Eula, who is the unself-conscious and almost mindless personification of the fecundity of nature, are almost like goddess and ogre, a positive and negative power, and the yoking of them together takes on the quality of an allegorical event. What keeps the story from becoming transparent allegory, and thus a too-bald commentary on the modern scene, is the richness of detail and the sheer power of fact which locate these two creatures in a community that is still close enough to nature to have nymphs and trolls walk within it and not so self-conscious as to have to rationalize them out of existence. [I thought of the community in which I grew up.]

What Faulkner achieves in *The Hamlet*, I decided, is to create archetypal characters that represent both group tradition and universal situations. By presenting them through the concrete particularities of a specific, individualized setting, though, he is able to delineate reality, the end of all great art, and not make some comment about the state of the modern world, as he does in *Intruder*, which is the function of rhetoric or propaganda.

The Town proved disappointing as a sequel to *The Hamlet*. Flem and Eula move into Jefferson to operate the hamburger restaurant Flem has won from Ratliff, and become embroiled in the mundane affairs of small-town life, thus losing their mythic quality. Eula cooks hamburgers and has an affair with Manfred de Spain, the mayor of the town, while Flem, taking advantage of his wife's infidelity and through bribery and intimidation, moves toward respectability by becoming, first, manager of the local water works, then vice-president and president of the Sartoris bank. Eula has been reduced from a character embodying the essence of femininity to a frustrated, unfulfilled middle-class housewife seeking her thrills by pitting Gavin Stevens against Manfred de Spain. Like so many other modern men and women, her life, totally lacking aim or purpose, leads inevitably to suicide. Flem's existence becomes a vicious parody of the modern success story.

On his way to affluence and power, Flem employs Benjamin Franklin's industry and frugality but adds to these traditional virtues the amoral ingenuity of the nineteenth-century robber baron. He has a monopoly on that which the wealthy and powerful want—Eula's body—and he sells it to the highest bidder. Luckily, he does not feel the need of it himself or the loss of it when it is gone. *The Town*, I decided, is not as bad a novel as *Main Street;* but the intent of the two novels is the same: both make a comment on modern society, a world that has lost its sense of mission, one obsessed with money, power, and respectability (or, at least, the appearance of it). Both novels are persuasive documents of social protest, but they are not, in my opinion, great art.

The Mansion does not sink to the level of *The Town* because, in the former—or at least part of it—Faulkner recaptures some of the spirit and atmosphere of *The Hamlet*. The last book in the Snopes trilogy is rescued from mediocrity by its concern with Mink Snopes' determination to wreak vengeance on Flem Snopes for allowing him to spend most of his life in prison. Like Flem and Eula in *The Hamlet,* Mink becomes an archetypal character representing a universal human trait—the desire to revenge a wrong he has received—but he is presented in specific, concrete, highly individualized terms. His desire for what he calls justice totally alienates him from his family. His every thought in prison is focused on his next meeting with Flem, and for thirty-eight years he fights off the daily temptation to spend his meager allowance on soda pop—his desire for it is, as Benjamin Franklin would say, the most pronounced erratum of his life—so that he will be prepared for his next confrontation with Flem. Mink is not modern man, for his is a life with a purpose, one for which he is willing to sacrifice everything else to accomplish a specific objective. Mink so dominates the novel that he is usually able to keep it above the level of mediocrity to which it constantly threatens to sink.

The creation of one excellent character—especially since the book contains little of *The Hamlet*'s authentic humor—does not completely offset the effect of Faulkner's didactic talk about the state of American society and that of the world in general; but it does make *The Mansion* a better book than *The Town*. More important, the appearance of the novel gave me cause for hope that Faulkner had not entirely lost his creative powers, and I awaited Faulkner's next book with great impatience.

I had to wait seven years, but *The Reivers* was worth the wait. Again, Faulkner is concerned with a universal archetypal action—a youth's initiation into manhood. The novel is filled with highly individualized characters, specific concrete settings, and serious situations made tolerable and memorable by infectious humor. It confirmed me in my conviction, one I reached after more than two decades of studying American literature, that one can not make a list of the five most important writers of American fiction without placing William Faulkner near the top of the list. This, Faulkner's last work, reminds the reader of two basic thematic concerns of his: deep respect for humanity's ability to endure, and their capacity for both good and evil.

What Malcolm Cowley did for Faulkner's reputation need not be rehearsed in detail here. Cowley rescued Faulkner from oblivion and made serious students of American literature read his great novels. Today more theses, dissertations, essays, and books are written about Faulkner than about any other American writer. It is commonplace to hear what I have been saying to my classes for a good many years, that Hawthorne, Melville, and Twain each wrote one book that possibly is the equal of Faulkner's best, but that Faulkner wrote six or seven others almost as good as his best.

One of the best craftsmen American fiction has ever produced was Henry James, but Faulkner's experiments in how a novel should be written (no two of his novels are cast in the same form) have been just as influential on the development of the technique of the modern novel as were those of James. That such statements go unquestioned today is a logical consequence of the initial impetus given Faulkner's fiction by *The Portable Faulkner.*

Over the years, however, as I have read Faulkner and worried about the apparent coincidence of the decline of his impressive creativity and the appearance of an essay that made American readers and critics aware of that creativity, I have come to the conclusion that these two events might not be so coincidental after all. The appearance of Cowley's essay/introduction suggests that there might be a reason for the decline in creative power. In 1945, Faulkner wrote Cowley about the progress of *The Hamlet:*

> Meanwhile my book had created Snopes and his clan, who produced stories in their saga which are to fall in a later volume. . . . [O]ne day I decided I had better start on the first volume or I'd never get any of it down. So I wrote an induction toward the spotted horse story, which included "Barn Burning" and "Wash," which I discovered had no place

in that book at all. "Spotted horses" became a longer story, picked up the HOUND (rewritten and much longer and with the character's name changed from Cotton to Snopes) and went on with JAMSHYD'S COURTYARD.

This is one of several justly famous statements made by Faulkner describing how his mind worked, how he took from the attic whatever "lumber" he needed to build the "chicken coop" he happened to be working on at the time. He never began with a plot but with a character, and used whatever material he could find or create to flesh out that character.

Another, equally informative explanation of how he wrote is included in the *Paris Review* interview with Jean Stein:

> I wrote [*The Sound and the Fury*] five separate times, trying to tell the story, to rid myself of the dream which would continue to anguish me until I did. . . . It began with a mental picture. I did not realize at the time it was symbolical. The picture was of the muddy seat of a little girl's drawers in a pear tree, where she could see through a window where her grandmother's funeral was taking place and report what was happening to her brothers on the ground below.

As Cowley wrote fifteen years after publication of *The Portable Faulkner,* Faulkner's letters to him at the time Cowley was preparing the volume for publication convinced him that in creating his characters, Faulkner "thought back to archetypes" and that he "tried to present characters rather than ideas." In the introduction to *The Portable Faulkner,* however, Cowley writes that Faulkner had created the history of a mythical county from the late eighteenth to the mid-twentieth century. The part of history that is missing is that of the third and fourth decades of the present century, a climactic portion of the saga, since it covers the period during which the Snopeses finally wrest control of Yoknapatawpha from the Sartorises. Cowley urged Faulkner to complete "the still unfinished Snopes saga," a suggestion which might have thrown

Faulkner's creative powers off track and made it possible for him to produce the two inferior novels in the Snopes trilogy.

Cowley's comments here might be interpreted as suggesting that Faulkner's novels create a more or less consistent, chronological development of a mythical county that stands as a metaphor for the Deep South. Faulkner might then have been moved to attempt to supply the missing link. He set about writing *The Town* and *The Mansion* to explain how Snopesism became the dominant force in Jefferson and throughout Yoknapatawpha County. As he described the victory of material acquisitiveness in his mythical kingdom, Faulkner made some perceptive yet troubling comments on the plight of the modern world. He then forgot his own credo, that the only subject worth writing about is the "human heart in conflict with itself." Donald Davidson once told me,

> William Faulkner the novelist is our noblest genius, and we should treat his great books as the precious objects they are; but William Faulkner the man, the poet, the essayist, the social critic is fallible like the rest of us, and he should be received in those roles with that fact fully recorded in our mind. Whatever the reasons for his devoting the forties and fifties to the kind of activities he did . . . we can forgive him, for we understand human frailty. After all, no one can take from us *The Sound and the Fury, Absalom, Absalom!, As I Lay Dying, Light in August, The Hamlet,* and *Go Down, Moses.*

CHAPTER
9

A Kind of Doctor that Can't Do Anyone Any Good

After a year as an instructor at the University of Mississippi, I resigned and, on the strong recommendation of Alton Bryant, Harry Campbell, and Ruel Foster, went to Vanderbilt University to begin work on my Ph.D. Having decided that I wanted to teach, I also decided to study at a university with strong ties to the Southern tradition. As Harry Campbell told me while I was studying for my master's, Vanderbilt was in large part responsible for the modern renaissance in Southern letters. Three of the most important literary movements in the United States in this century originated there.

In the first of these movements, a group of young poets had attempted to replace the sentimentality of nineteenth-century Southern poetry with what came to be called "high modernism." The association of a group of Vanderbilt students and faculty had begun about 1913 as informal social meetings and by 1916 had developed into a group of faculty members, students, and townspeople who met to discuss in more detail than formal classes permitted (or allowed) such religious and philosophical issues as the effect of Higher Criticism on established religion. Soon after World War I, the group—by then consisting of John Crowe Ransom, Donald Davidson, William Elliott, Jesse Wills, Ridley Wills, Alec B. Stevenson, Merrill Moore, Sidney Hirsh, James M. Frank, and Stanley Johnson—resumed its meetings. Gradually, Ransom, who in 1919 had published *Poems About God,* assumed leadership, and the group discussions began to concentrate on the technique of poetry. Before long, Robert Penn Warren, William Frierson, and Allen Tate were members, and the group began holding regular meetings at the home of James M. Frank. According to Donald Davidson, these meetings were serious attempts to learn as much as could be learned about the craft of poetry:

> First, we gave strict attention from the beginning to the *form* of poetry. . . . Every poem was read aloud by the poet himself, while the members of the group had before them typed copies of the poem. . . . [After the reading] the discussion began, and it was likely to be ruthless in its exposure of any technical weakness as to rhyme, meter imagery, metaphor and was often minute in analysis of details.

From April 1922 to December 1925, *The Fugitive* published nineteen issues and included most of John Crowe Ransom's best verse. It had a great influence in shaping the careers of Tate, Davidson, and Warren. After 1925, the meetings of the poets became less frequent. Many of the group's members had left Nashville. Tate was in New York doing free-lance journalism, and Warren was in California attending graduate school, but they remained active enough to bring out in 1928 *The Fugitives: An Anthology of Verse.* About half of the ninety-four poems that appeared in the volume had been reprinted from the *Fugitive;* the remainder were reprinted from other magazines. *Fugitives* did, however, include some poems written by the Fugitives since the magazine had ceased publication.

The movement had produced four poets of power and lasting importance: Ransom, Tate, Warren, and Davidson. Between 1925 and 1928, some of the Fugitives who had previously devoted their time and energy to poetry became interested in other matters and shifted to criticism of political, social, and cultural issues. "I can hardly speak for the others," said Davidson, writing in 1957 about the Scopes trial in 1925,

> but for John Ransom and myself . . . it was horrifying to see the cause of liberal education argued in a Tennessee court by a famous agnostic lawyer named Clarence Darrow. It was still more horrifying—and frightening—to realize that the South was being exposed to large-scale public detraction and did not know, or much care, how to answer.

Soon, Allen Tate, Robert Penn Warren, and Andrew Lytle joined Ransom and Davidson, and they decided to gather kindred spirits to their cause and formulate an answer to the region's detractors: John Gould Fletcher, H. B. Kline, Lyle Lanier, Stark Young, H. C. Nixon, F. L. Owsley, and John Donald Wade. Together, they formed the Agrarians and in 1930 issued *I'll Take My Stand,* surely one of the most significant books of its kind ever produced in this country. Some Agrarians joined others generally sympathetic to their point of view and published *Who Owns America?* (1938).

The third important literary movement to come out of the intellectual ferment at Vanderbilt was the New Criticism. This way of reading literature, especially poetry, has had a profound impact on the way in which poems are read today. The movement had its beginning in Ransom's way of reading poetry in his classes and in the kind of details emphasized by the Fugitives. The critical impact of the New Critics was so widespread that, after 1945, few poetry classes were taught like the Romantic poetry class I'd had as an undergraduate.

Among the first courses I signed up for was Reading Poetry. The man who taught the course, Donald Davidson, announced that in the course he would follow the principles of the New Criticism. He had therefore placed on reserve critical books by John Crowe Ransom and by three of Ransom's best-known students, Tate, Warren, and Brooks. The text in the course was Cleanth Brooks' *The Well-Wrought Urn*. After the first few lectures, I began to understand the difference between the course in the Romantic poets I had had in college and Wilson's lectures on Shakespeare at Stratford. Davidson read the definition of poetry from Ransom's *The World's Body*: "Poetry is the kind of knowledge by which we must know what we have arranged that we cannot know otherwise." If poetry is to reveal to us the unique quality of knowledge it possesses, Davidson assured us, poetry must be read *as poetry* and not as biography, history, homiletics, or psychology. I suddenly realized that in Romantic poetry, I had acquired a great deal of fascinating information about the poets—without having read critically the poetry itself. On the other hand, Professor Wilson had made me read and had helped me interpret the poetry of Shakespeare's plays. That was the difference between the two classes. In one, the students read the literature; in the other, they read about the men who had created the literature. The professor in the poetry course assured his class that they were going to read the poetry and not about the authors or the times in which they lived. I was excited. Right then and there, I began to believe that I had chosen the right profession. Nothing could be more exciting or rewarding than reading good books, then talking and writing about them. What a way to earn a living!

As the class read the poems in the text—which ranged from Donne's "The Canonization" through Milton's "L'Allegro" and "Il Penseroso," Gray's "Elegy Written in a Country Church-Yard," Wordsworth's "Ode: Intimations of Immortality Recollected from Early Childhood," and ended with Yeats' "Among School Children"—the instructor insisted that the class read the poem and not accept any of the three usual substitutions offered for it: (1) a paraphrase of its logical or narrative content (2) a study of the poet's biography or the history of the age in which he lived, or (3) an inspirational or didactic interpretation. Although a prose paraphrase of a poem may sometimes be useful, I learned, in getting to know what the poem is about or gaining a knowledge of the poet's life and the times in which he lived may aid in experiencing the work of art, such information must be kept in the subordinate and preliminary position it reasonably occupies. It must never be accepted as a substitute for the poem itself. Modern man has little knowledge of the world in which he lives except that which he learns through scientific observation. His perception of the world is incomplete; therefore it is faulty. If one knows only what science reveals, he is ignorant of the body and solid substance of the world; he is unaware that the world is made of "whole and indivisible objects." The only means by which man can recover the concrete actuals of the real world from his memory, to which they have retired, is through poetry. Poetry, I learned, contains a quality or order of knowledge distinct from the quality one achieves through science. It is the only means by which one can know the concrete particularities of the world's body. The function of poetry, Davidson insisted, is neither didactic nor inspirational; it is cognitive. He was not content that his students understand poetry's cognitive function as they came to perceive how a poem differs from an expository essay; they should know that the difference lies in both the order of knowledge the poem presents and its basic structure.

"The structure of a poem," the class read in Ransom's *The New Criticism*, "is the prose of the poem, being a logical discourse of almost any kind." It includes a beginning, a middle, and an end; like any other "argument," it may be stated completely in prose. The "texture" is so "free, unrestricted, and large" that it cannot be included in the structure. Many readers of poetry are satisfied with its structure, which they quickly reduce to a didactic or inspirational prose statement and thus think they "have" the poem. But they do not, Ransom warns. They have omitted its texture (its tropes, allusions, and connotations) and thus have missed the order of knowledge the poetry provides: the recovery of the "denser and more refractory original world" that we know through "our perception and memories."

After Davidson's course, I thought that for the first time I understood the nature and function of poetry, how this nature and function differ from the nature and function of expository prose—for the first time. What I did not know was that I had just had an introduction to the approach to literature that was to revolutionize the way the subject was taught to two generations of students. I studied carefully the poetry of Keats and Wordsworth and learned that they were better poets than Byron, even if they were less mystifying men.

At Vanderbilt, I had other excellent teachers. One of them was Walter Clyde Curry, an old-line scholar who taught me medieval literature. Because I knew nothing about medieval literature, and because I could hardly read Middle English, I was delighted that Curry concentrated first on the language, telling us just how medieval poetry influenced later poets. Medieval literature was also an introduction to graduate study. One day Professor Curry said to the class: "You are now in professional school. We are trying to train you to be scholar-teachers and only you can allow us to succeed in our attempt. I can illustrate what I mean by giving you some personal information. After my wife and I had decided to marry, we had a long conversation one afternoon. I don't ever want to own a home, I told her; so we can live in my apartment or yours. I don't care which. You decide. I determined several years ago that I wanted to wear in winter blue serge suits (and in summer tan linen), blue-and-white striped ties, blue socks, and black shoes. Joseph Frank and Sons [a downtown clothier] knows my preferences and needs, so he sends me my requirements automatically each year. Finally, I like to eat almost anything, so you decide what we're going to have for dinner each day. If you can't decide, I like ground round steak. Ladies and gentlemen, that conversation took almost the entire afternoon, but I have always thought it was time well spent because I have never since that afternoon had to give a moment's thought to food, clothing, and shelter. I have thought about scholarship. You have to decide if you want to be a scholar enough to be one. I always used that story when I taught Thoreau's *Walden*. The only way to decide upon the essentials of life is to determine how 'much of this thing called life you have to exchange for it.'"

I met Professor Curry one afternoon in 1962, after I had returned to Vanderbilt to teach. He was retired, and I hadn't seen him in ten years. Doubting that he would remember me, I put out my hand and said, "Professor Curry, I'm Dan Young."

"Oh, yes," he said, "Mr. Young. I remember you. You're on too many committees. When I was chairman, I listed the committees I was on, and the list covered almost two pages. I added a sentence to the list and sent it to the dean: 'I hereby resign from all the above committees.' Then I had time to finish my Milton book." Curry had once said that he'd decided early in his career that he would write an important book on the greatest poets in the English language—Chaucer, Milton, and Shakespeare—and he had done just that.

During my first year at Vanderbilt, I took a full load of course work. Since I had the Shakespeare credit, I could have taken a light load each term; but I wanted to save that extra time to work on my dissertation. During that first year, I used every available moment to study for the preliminary examination. I'd had an examination much like it before I received my master's from the University of Mississippi, and I continued the study I had begun for it through the summer.

In mid-October, I signed up to take the examination during the spring semester of my first year—a year early. Most students took the examination during the second semester of their second year.

Unsure when the exam would be, I continued to study. One Monday in April 1949, as I passed Professor Curry's office, he motioned for me to come in. "I've scheduled your examination for seven o'clock Wednesday," he said. "Don't be late." I promised that I wouldn't. Guessing that Beatty (my major professor) didn't know the time of the exam, I went down the hall to tell him. It was Professor Curry's habit to notify the faculty in person, not to issue memoranda. He was proud of the fact that in his twenty years as chairman, he'd never held a faculty meeting.

Professor Beatty asked me on which writer I'd like the questioning to begin (as my major professor, the one with whom I had already arranged to write my dissertation, Beatty would begin the questioning). I thought for a moment, then answered: Thoreau.

When, two days later, Professor Curry declared the examination officially open, I was all set with a pat explanation of "Civil Disobedience," which I thought was Beatty's favorite work by Thoreau. Instead, Beatty turned to me and asked about *Mr. Blanding Builds His Dream House*. "In this novel, Mr. Young, the house has been completed, and Mr. Blanding walks in it for the first time. He goes directly to the bathroom and flushes the commode, expecting to hear the sound Arnold heard on Dover Beach. Can you explain this allusion?" To this day, I cannot reconstruct my reply. The question was about as far from what I had expected as it could possibly be. Although I hadn't read *Mr. Blanding*, I knew Arnold's poem; so I took a stab at an answer. When I finished, Professor Beatty merely said "good" and went on to ask me about "Civil Disobedience." My confidence somewhat restored, the questioning then went to Professor Curry, whose questions were easier than I had expected.

For the next two hours I spent as much time saying "I don't know" as I did trying to answer questions. Finally dismissed, I was asked to wait in a classroom down the hall. I went there and sat down, trying to decide how best to prepare for the next examination. After what seemed an eternity, I heard a faint noise and looked up. Professor Beatty was coming in the door. With a big smile, Beatty said: "Congratulations! That was some performance!" We went back to the examination room, where the others congratulated me; then I was dismissed. Somehow I made my way home to a roomful of friends who had had more confidence in my ability than I. They had come to celebrate with me, and that we did, although I was pleased that none of them had witnessed my performance.

"What was going on at your house last night," a neighbor asked the next day. "Did someone die?"

"No," I said, "someone was born," and "we were celebrating his birth."

The requirements for the seminars were similar. Each semester every student made a report on a subject assigned by the instructor. After a conference with the professor, the student wrote a fuller account of the subject, making sure all the important scholarship had been included. The paper was turned in, and the student was finished until the final exam.

One afternoon after the examination, the members of one of the seminars were invited to the professor's house for dinner. Usually these invitations came a week or ten days after the seminar was completed and the examinations were over. This professor was violating the custom, since he had to leave the next day to teach summer school. Soon after we arrived and were settled in picnic chairs around the pool, a shower came up. We rushed inside, but the shower lasted only a few minutes; so we went back outside. Now the chairs were too wet, whereupon the professor's wife told her husband to get some paper to cover the seats of the chairs. He went inside and returned with paper—the papers we had spent most of the afternoon writing. The chairs were dully lined, and the professor invited us to have a seat. We did. I (and probably, most of the

A Kind of Doctor that Can't Do Anyone Any Good

others) spent the rest of the evening trying to see, without being noticed, whose paper I was sitting on. I finally spotted the name; the paper belonged to a good friend of mine. But—and I asked several—I couldn't find out who was sitting on *my* paper. To put a cap on the mystery, we picked up the soggy papers and put them in the garbage before leaving. The professor left for California, and a few days later we received our grades. As far as I could determine, everyone received the grade he had expected. Each of those present at the party had several seminars with this particular professor. I suspect he had a good idea of the quality of our work without even reading the papers.

As soon as I had completed the qualifying examination, I began to think seriously about my dissertation topic. I had already asked Professor Richmond Croom Beatty to suggest a topic in modern American literature, my chosen field. He suggested "Fiction in the Era of Social Protest." From that moment, every time I got a chance in the American literature seminar or the American intellectual history course, I selected a seminar report that would allow me to read and write in that period. During my first year I did two reports in the literature class and three in the history class. Since I had done my thesis on the political and social thought of Jack London, the field wasn't brand new to me, and by the end of the first year I had a good start on my dissertation.

It wasn't that I was trying to rush through my graduate program; I was just trying to finish before my money ran out. I was receiving $110 a month from the G.I. Bill and $1,000 a year for teaching a section of freshman English. Even in 1948, it wasn't easy to live on that. Our family had grown to four. Our first son, Thomas Daniel Young, Jr., was born October 11, 1947, before we left the University of Mississippi, and our second, Terry Lewis Young, came on October 31, 1948, soon after we arrived at Vanderbilt.

In the summer of 1949, I had no classes to take or teach and was able to devote full time to the dissertation. So I wouldn't be disturbed, Arlease took the two boys and spent the summer at her parents' home in Rose Hill, Mississippi. By devoting every hour I could stay awake to the project, including Sundays, I had completed a draft by September 15 and could spend two weeks with them before returning to Vanderbilt for the fall term. During the fall and early part of the winter quarter, I read and polished the manuscript, then gave it to a typist. I then gave the typed manuscript to Professor Beatty to read. About two weeks later, he reported that it had been approved by the committee and that my defense was set for the last week of the quarter.

The defense was a genuine pleasure. It became apparent to me that everyone on the committee was convinced that I knew more about my topic than any one living, and they were merely trying to learn what they could from the pro forma exercise. After about an hour, Professor Beatty asked if anyone had any other questions. No one did, so I was excused. Professor Curry soon came into the room and, as was his custom on such occasions, stuck out his hand and said, "Let me be the first to congratulate you—*Doctor* Young." To which Professor Beatty quickly responded: "Not so fast, Doctor Curry. The man has another quarter of course work to complete." I worried for several days, wondering if Professor Curry would force me to defend the dissertation *again* after I had finished my course work. But after Curry's initial look of astonishment and a startled "What!" the subject was never mentioned again.

I was delighted when Professor Curry mentioned at a meeting of the Graduate English Club that I had earned the Ph.D. in record time—from September 1948 to June 1950. It was even more pleasing to be offered a teaching position at my alma mater—then Mississippi Southern College, now the University of Southern Mississippi. My family and I went through my home community on our way to the new position, and while we were there, Barkstol stopped by. He was, of course, looking for a lift to Possum Hollow. My father informed Barkstol that after more than twenty years of schooling, I had earned my doctorate and was now a doctor.

"I'll swany," he said. "You know, I would never athought it 'cause it don't seem that education had changed ol' Dan a bit. Are you goin' in partners with Doc?"

"No," my father replied; "Dan is a kind of doctor that can't do anyone any good."

Maybe so, I thought, *but I have helped myself a lot.*

CHAPTER

10

I Hear You Got Hired

The opportunity to return to teach at my alma mater and to be near Arlease's family delighted us. Adding to our pleasure, we unexpectedly came upon enough money to buy a new car (our 1940 Ford coupe had become rather cramped for four). The Air Force came to our rescue.

One day about a month before graduation, I received a letter informing me that I was to be paid for my unused leave time while in service. Since I had served three years and nine months, and since I was due thirty days leave each year, the amount would be almost $2,000—enough for us to buy the car *and* furnish a small house in Hattiesburg.

With great glee, Arlease carted most of what had passed for our furniture to the city dump, and we left Nashville in a 1950 Ford sedan, with enough money left over to pay the moving van and furnish the house on Seventh Avenue in Hattiesburg that we had rented. Even on an annual salary of $3,600, we could afford an entire house. It was near school and faced a large cemetery, and all our neighbors lived there, it seemed, because they could not afford a house in any other neighborhood.

After getting the furniture, clothes, and books unloaded, we left for a ten-day visit with Arlease's family. We returned to Hattiesburg just before summer school opened. Arlease and a friend of hers went furniture shopping while I got acquainted with my new colleagues. I spent some time with Richard Aubrey McLemore, dean of the college, and inspected the library (which I found disappointing, since it contained few of the books and journals I would need for the work I wanted to do). I knew the head of the department, W. W. Stout, only by reputation. Stout had been a student of Paul Green's at the University of North Carolina. While at Southern, I had appeared in one of Stout's dramas, "Dinner in Carter's Kitchen." Thus, I anticipated meeting not only a real live writer but a writer who was a colleague.

On Monday, then, I could hardly wait to reach his office. I knocked and, after "Come in," went in. Stout was seated at a desk. Ignoring my outstretched hand, he neither raised his head or his hand, but instead put a key in my hand and said: "I hear you got hired. You'll have a desk in the room next door." He dismissed me by turning his back and continuing with what he had been doing when I entered.

The room containing my "desk" was the size of a classroom. It held twelve desks, each with a hard-bottomed chair. On one side of each desk was a cane-bottomed chair (for student consultations) and on the other, a small bookcase. There were ten middle-aged women and one man in the room. I made the rounds, introducing myself, then asked if anyone knew which was my desk. They all drew a blank; apparently, Professor Stout hadn't notified them of my coming. The lone man, Leon Eubanks, said he thought a desk at the back was vacant. Finding the desk in question, I emptied the contents of my briefcase in the drawers, then returned to the car for a carton of books. I returned to find a student seated at my desk. As I put the carton down, the student asked: "Are you Doctor Young?" I said I was. "Doctor Stout wants to see you."

This time, Professor Stout was more cordial. He handed me a sheet of paper containing a schedule of three freshman English classes. "You see," he said, "I've given you a reduced load [most of the instructors had four classes]. You and I will teach the advanced students. All the advanced students are taught tutorially. Would you rather have pre-Renaissance or post-Renaissance?"

Professor Stout was asking me—who had concentrated on twentieth-century American literature in graduate school—whether I would rather teach Beowulf, Chaucer, Milton, Spenser; or John Donne and the metaphysical poets, the Cavalier poets, Pope, Swift, Dryden, eighteenth-century drama, Wordsworth, Shelley, Byron, Keats, Arnold, Tennyson, the other Victorians, and the modern British writers. I knew little about either group but reluctantly chose the latter, thinking I might find someone who wanted to read Faulkner, Ransom, Eliot, Pound, William Carlos Williams, Hemingway, Fitzgerald, or Stevens—in other words, writers I knew something about.

By talking to some of my colleagues, I learned that freshman English was taught in an unusual manner. One week, students sat in class and listened to classical music piped in from Professor Stout's office; the next week, they wrote and submitted their impressions of what they had heard the previous week. Unfortunately, few of them had much to write—they had slept through most of the music.

After two days of receiving papers repeating such attitudes as "I thought it was real pretty, but I could never understand that kind of music," or "It sounded good, but it didn't seem to have a tune. It sure would have been hard to dance by," I disconnected the speakers in my room. I tried to convince my students of the importance of their being able to express themselves. We reviewed the principles of grammar and discussed the ways to develop a paragraph. I brought an apple to class and asked them to describe it—what it looked like, how it felt in their hands, what it tasted like—anything descriptive they could think of to write down. Eventually, Professor Stout realized that my classes were no longer listening to music. He didn't say a word; he simply disconnected *me* from the course.

I had only two or three majors. Before long, they came by to see me, complaining that they "just did not understand poetry." Without fail, I followed the same routine. I had them read several of the better-known Metaphysical poems: then, together, we discussed the poems, eventually moving on to Eliot's discussion of the "objective correlative" and Ransom's "meant metaphor." After several weeks of close discussion and careful reading of the poems, we read "The Love Song of J. Alfred Prufrock" and "The Equilibrists." I attempted to demonstrate how poetry differs from prose and why, as Ransom says, "poetry is the means by which we know that which we have arranged that we cannot know otherwise." I was actually aware that only the brightest students could make sense of what I was trying to do; the others either did not show up for their appointments or attempted simpler verse.

As the quarter wore on, I became more and more dissatisfied. I became thoroughly convinced that I would never be satisfied in such a chaotic system. One Sunday afternoon, I called Dean McLemore and made an appointment to see him in his office the following morning. At nine o'clock the next morning, I went to McLemore's office and told him as specifically as I could of my dissatisfaction and the reasons for it. I promised to stay until the end of the summer; but during that time I would be trying desperately to find another position for the fall. Dean McLemore asked me to promise him that I would make no final commitment until we had talked again, to which I agreed. I continued to teach as best I could, while reading proof for *The Literature of the South,* which I, Professor Beatty, and Floyd C. Watkins of Emory University, had edited.

About two weeks later, Dean McLemore called me at home and asked me to meet him and President Cook at 7:30 the following morning. As I hung up the phone, I could think of no reason why they wanted to see me other than to try to persuade me to stay. But I had already determined to leave at the end of the term. In fact, I had written a letter to Lincoln Memorial University, asking whether the position I had been offered earlier was still open. What I was not expecting was the conversation that transpired the next morning in President Cook's office.

Dean McLemore and I went across the hall to the president's office. Doctor Cook, whom I had known briefly as Captain Cook in Special Services in the Air Force, received us cordially. What he had to say overwhelmed me. "When we hired you," he said, "Doctor Mac and I intended to offer you the chairmanship of the department if you worked out as well as we expected. Now, with this unexpected turn of events, we are prepared to make you a new offer."

The "new offer" went as follows. I would become chairman of the department on September 1. I would be promoted to professor of English, given tenure (usually the school required five years of service before one's position became permanent). I would receive $4,800 a year (a raise of $1,200) and a supplement of $1,200 if I taught in the summer session (a raise of $300). If I wished, I could teach one night course to veterans each term. My regular teaching load would be one course per term. All this added up to a $2,700-a-year raise. With Dean McLemore's approval, I could restructure the department any way I chose. Dean McLemore assured me that he wanted the department to be modeled on Vanderbilt's (he had taken a Ph.D. in history there). Realizing that I would need more Ph.D.s, he promised to help me any way he could to attract the people I wanted. Both men assured me they would provide the funds for me to improve the library's holdings of books in my field.

What President Cook and Dean McLemore wanted, they insisted, was for me to wait patiently through the summer. Doctor Cook would notify Professor Stout, and I could talk to Stout about what position he would hold in the department. But, Cook reminded me, Stout had tenure; so his membership on the faculty was secure.

It took me about five minutes to accept the offer. When I'd done so, I went straight to the office and wrote Professor Byno Rhodes, chairman of the department at Lincoln Memorial, asking him to disregard my recent letter. For the rest of the summer, I taught my classes, read proof for the anthology, and spent the rest of my time rewriting the English-department section of the college catalogue, trying to make it as conventional and conservative as I could. The first-year course was English composition. The sophomore course was Introduction to Literature; and the required text was *An Approach to Literature* by Brooks, Purser, and Warren, supplemented by one paperback novel each term. By then, the term was over, and I took the family to Rose Hill for a vacation with Arlease's parents.

Upon my return to Hattiesburg, I found a note in my post office box from Dean McLemore, informing me that my office was Room 201, in College Hall. When I went over to inspect my new quarters, I found that the old room I had shared with eleven others had been subdivided into six spaces. The first office had been divided into a small, outer office for a secretary, with my office immediately behind. The other offices would house two professors each. Professor Stout's office was undisturbed. I looked on my desk and there saw the biggest ring of keys I'd ever seen. They were the only evidence I ever had that Professor Stout had turned the mantle of leadership over to me.

Before registration for the new quarter began, I sent out temporary, mimeographed descriptions of the new courses. On this schedule I listed: "Tutorial in English literature, variable credit; sixteen hours may be counted toward a major in English, Professor Stout." For myself, I listed a course in the modern novel.

The schedule duly appeared, and Professor Stout sent word by a student that he wanted to see me. Certain that he would complain about the schedule, I went to his office. The schedule was never mentioned. "I've been looking at an advance copy of *The Literature of the South*," he said, "and I was surprised to see that so many of the writers are from Mississippi. I think we should do a literary map of the state." After some more conversation, we concluded that we would get an art student we both knew, named George Robertson, to do the illustrations. I would describe a scene from the writer's work that I thought would properly illustrate that writer's contribution to American literature. Meanwhile, Stout would supervise printing and distribution. Thus was born "The Literature Map of Mississippi."

Robertson came by to see me, and I described a scene from a work by each author that I thought would be representative of the writer's work (for example, the hanging scene from Faulkner's "Dry September"), or a character (a Southern colonel for Percy's *Lanterns on the Levee*). I was amazed at the quality of George's work. I told him to place the illustrations on a map of Mississippi at the approximate location of the authors' hometowns. I later learned that Stout had suggested some symbolic images of Mississippi for George to use on the border—cotton boll, steamship, hunter, and so on. Stout sent him back to me for a bibliography of works to be represented, and I didn't see the map again until its completion and a thousand copies had been printed. I admired the finished product. A professional job, it nevertheless contained some glaring errors (for "Elizabeth *Spencer*" he wrote *Spenser*, and for "*Irwin* Russell," *Irving*; and he placed Russell at Pascagoula, not Port Gibson, where he belonged). The map caught on despite these flaws. Recommended by the High School English section of the Mississippi Education Association, it was ordered by many schools and libraries. It made a fine gift, and at least two firms gave free copies with purchases of their products. By the time a second edition was needed, George had graduated and was a commercial artist somewhere in the Midwest; so the second edition carried the same three errors as the first edition.

While this project was in progress, I continued my effort to find and employ Ph.D.'s. I knew, for instance, that Ralph Hitt, a good friend from my Vanderbilt days, was dissatisfied with his position at Allegheny College. Another possibility was Henry O'Bannon. I had attended the University of Mississippi with O'Bannon and knew that, except for his dissertation, he'd finished his Ph.D. requirements. I also knew that he wanted a position with which to support his family while he finished writing the dissertation. With Dean McLemore's approval, I offered positions to both. In the meantime, I was writing catalogue descriptions for traditional courses in English and American literature.

When I left Mississippi Southern in 1957, I had ten Ph.D.s on the faculty and two others lined up. We had more than a hundred majors, and many of our best graduates were going on to graduate school, some after earning an M.A. with us. All members of the English Department spoke at nearby high schools, encouraging—not too obviously, we hoped—students to come to Southern, and their teachers to attend the special courses we were then offering on Saturday mornings. The school was rapidly increasing its enrollment (from about 1,700 in 1950 to 3,800 in 1957) and was becoming recognized as one of the three major colleges and universities in the state.

In the summer of 1957, I received an offer from Delta State University that I thought I shouldn't refuse. A substantial salary, plus a house with utilities and a telephone, were part of the offer. What kept me from accepting the position at once was that, when our son Kyle David was born four years earlier, we had built a new house, and I dreaded having to sell it on such short notice.

I was having morning coffee with R. G. Lowrey, a colleague, shortly after the offer from Delta State and mentioned I was thinking of selling my house (I did not say why). In a casual tone of voice, Lowrey asked how much I wanted for it. Aware that real estate near the campus was becoming more expensive, I nonchalantly said: "Three thousand down, and the buyer can take up the payments.

"How much cash would you require?"

"Oh," I said, still thinking his interest was casual, "ninety-five hundred."

"I'll take it. I believe Leonard [his son] and his family would like to live there."

We finished our coffee and went back to our respective offices. I busied myself with other matters. About ten minutes later, Lowrey came into my office, held out a check for $9,500, and asked where the deed was. "In a bank vault," I said.

"Let's go get it."

I was flabbergasted. It hadn't occurred to me that he would buy the house before Leonard and his wife looked it over. Even if Lowrey's son and daughter-in-law liked the house, I thought, it would take time for Lowrey to raise the money.

Obviously, that wasn't the case. We went to the bank and got the deed. I gave him a check to pay off the balance owed on the house, signed the title, and deposited his check in my account. Then I went home and told Arlease what had happened. In a few minutes, I was talking to President J. M. Ewing, accepting his offer of a position as professor of English and dean of the college at Delta State. I was thirty-eight years old and had been out of the Air Force almost eleven years.

The dean's house was excellent. Of tan stucco with a red-tiled roof, it had a large eat-in kitchen, a formal dining room, a large living room, three bedrooms, two baths, a study, a small porch, and a large patio; above the garage were a guest bedroom and bath. The house had central heat and air-conditioning.

Delta State differed from all the other schools I'd been associated with. Since its founding in 1924, the school had been Delta State Teachers' College, and, despite the change of name, still had as its primary objective training teachers for public schools. Still a small school, it had yet to enroll its five hundredth student. Our objective during my first year at Delta State was to exceed that figure. We enrolled 527.

We liked Cleveland very much. Yet, looking back on that period of my life, I realize now that it was also the most troubled period of my career. The problem was, I was torn between my duties as dean and those as a teacher. Every semester I insisted that Professor Hitt (who had come with me from Southern as head of the English Department) assign me a class. At the same time, Floyd Watkins and I were collaborating on a book of Faulkner criticism. My situation can be reduced to the simple statement that I was not doing *to my satisfaction* any of these three jobs. My attention was divided so badly that I couldn't attend to important matters in the dean's office. President Ewing had explained to me on my first day there that I was to be second in command; when he was away from the office (which, as things turned out, was frequently the case), I was responsible for all operations of the school. I was often called upon to make a decision without having sufficient information, energy, or interest on which to base the decision. As dean, I assisted department chairmen in recruiting suitable faculty. I advised the dean of men or the dean of women in determining the appropriate penalty for a student in violation of one or another social regulation. The registrar often called on me for assistance in ascertaining graduation requirements. Because I would not allow myself to become completely and solely involved in my position, I was at best a second-rate dean.

Then there was the matter of teaching. Teaching was what I had been trained to do. Now, I tended to carry the problems of the dean's office into the classroom. Seldom was I properly prepared to teach the novel, short story, poem, or essay under consideration. This situation led me to be a second-rate *teacher*.

Finally, I was committed to do half of a book on one of America's foremost literary figures. The only time left for this third task was after a tiring day at the office doing a job unrelated to writing or scholarship. Then, too, I had no time to go to other libraries for necessary source materials. I was able to complete only two of the six chapters I had agreed to write. Even more disgusted—*and* frustrated—I had to tell Floyd Watkins that I could not complete my part of the book, that he would have to do it alone.

I was feeling really low. What I should do next, give up my other activities and devote full time to the dean's office? Resign and return to the English Department? Resign and seek a position elsewhere? I doubted that I could do the first, and at Delta State the English Department did not offer the graduate courses and research opportunities I thought I needed.

I had just about decided on the third option when I went to New Orleans for a meeting of the Southern Association of Secondary Schools and Colleges. There, I saw Emmett Fields, with whom I had been in graduate school at Vanderbilt and who was now dean of Vanderbilt's College of Arts and Science. Emmett asked whether I had plans for dinner. I did not, and we arranged to meet at seven in the hotel's dining room. We were having coffee and brandy after a delicious dinner of Alaskan king crab when Emmett suddenly asked me: "What would you think of returning to Vanderbilt?"

"In what capacity?"

"Dean of Admissions."

This answer didn't completely satisfy me, so I asked: "Could I, at some point, return to teaching?"

Fields' reply—"Certainly, at the appropriate time"—was sufficiently encouraging to cause me to say I would be flattered by the chance to return to an academic institution with the reputation for excellence that Vanderbilt had.

"Good," Emmett said; "I'll recommend you to Vice-Chancellor Purdy."

CHAPTER
11

Do Not Go Beyond this Point Unless You Know the Way Is Clear

Arriving home, I was told that a man named Purdy from Nashville had called and wanted me to return his call as soon as possible. I went to the phone and called Purdy. He wanted to know how soon I could come to Nashville to discuss the position Dean Fields had mentioned. "Will tomorrow be soon enough?" I responded. "Great," he said. "I'll expect you at nine o'clock."

When I returned from New Orleans, I found something else—a renewal contract at Delta State. Since President Ewing had been more than fair to me, I thought it only fair that I discuss any other positions with him. As expected, he was very fair and generous. "If it's more money you want, I can meet any offer Vanderbilt can make."

I assured him that money was not the major concern. Then he gave me one of the greatest compliments I have ever received. Rising to shake my hand, he said: "I knew it was only a matter of time. You're too good for this position. For some time, I've been afraid that someone would discover it."

Leaving the president's office, I went by the house and had a bite of lunch; then I caught a plane to Nashville. The next morning, I went to Dean Fields' office and together we went down the hall to see Vice-Chancellor Purdy. After a cordial greeting, Purdy told me something about the position. First, Vanderbilt's undergraduate schools were receiving far more applicants than the university had openings. With the help of the admissions committee for each undergraduate school, he wanted strict criteria established so that the qualifications of each applicant could be measured effectively. I would serve as chairman of each admissions committee. Since there were already two full-time travelers in the office calling on the better schools around the country, I would not have to travel, just occasionally speak to alumni clubs which had invited groups of students to come learn more about Vanderbilt. In addition to chairing the admissions committees, I would be expected to arrange for student volunteers to show students and their parents around the campus and to speak to these students on behalf of Vanderbilt. The salary offered was $2,000 more than that which Delta State was then paying. On the other hand, Vanderbilt wasn't offering a free house and utilities. Arlease and I had already discussed one of the *disadvantages* of having a free house furnished: we might reach retirement with no place to live. But Doctor Purdy assured me that Vanderbilt would lend us the money to buy the house we wanted, at a very low rate of interest.

I was about to say I would accept the position. Then it occurred to me to bring up one last matter. "At Delta State, I have tenure. What would be my situation at Vanderbilt?"

Purdy picked up the phone and called Randall Stewart, chairman of the English Department. "Randall, if I were to employ Dan Young to help me, would you let him teach an English class occasionally if he wanted to, and could?"

"Of course, he could," Randall replied; "next spring I'll give him Southern literature, and he can use his own textbook."

Putting down the phone, Purdy turned back to me and said: "There's one other matter I forgot to mention. I need some help with the academic budgets of the undergraduate colleges. So your title will be Dean of Undergraduate Admissions and Assistant to the Vice-Chancellor, at a salary of fourteen thousand." I was to remain at Vanderbilt, in one capacity or another, for the next twenty-five years.

During my first semester at Vanderbilt, I learned my duties, met and talked with students, ran the office, escorted groups around the campus; *but I did not teach*. Then Randall Stewart offered me a most attractive situation. John Crowe Ransom had retired from Kenyon College and accepted a position as Visiting Distinguished Professor of English at Vanderbilt. Randall wondered if I would sit in on Ransom's class, call the roll, and grade his papers.

I couldn't have been more pleased. I had long considered Ransom one of the most important men of letters in modern America and was delighted to have the chance to get to know him. Then, too, Ransom badly needed me. With about a hundred students, he could not possibly grade all the papers that would be required from them. And calling the roll wasn't as easy and straightforward as it at first seemed. At that time, Vanderbilt had a complicated absence policy. Every student who was absent had to go to the dean's office and explain the absence. Depending on the reason, the student was given an excused or unexcused absence. This absence report had to be turned into the instructor before the student was allowed to return to class. At the end of the semester the instructor had to turn in the total student's absences (excused and unexcused), along with the instructor's grade report. The number of unexcused absences a student had accumulated could, and did, affect the student's grade in the course.

I did everything for Ransom that semester except the actual teaching. He would come into the classroom and speak to the students, then say: "We're here to read and talk about some poems. Let's start with the one on 257." He would read the poem quietly, with no explanation, and say: "What do you think of that one?" When someone said something, Ransom would nod or nod his head. "Good, let's read another." Then he might turn to Burns' "My Luv" and read it.

It slowly dawned on me that, unless someone asked a question, Ransom was prepared to read—without comment—for the entire semester. One day, I whispered to the girl next to me: "Ask him what he means by a 'meant metaphor.'" She did.

"I believe," Ransom responded, "I can best demonstrate what I mean by looking at a particular poem"; and he began reading Donne's "A Valediction: Forbidding Mourning." "The meant metaphor is," he said:

> If they [our souls] be two,
>   they are two so
> As stiff twin compasses are two;

He proceeded to demonstrate that all that goes before this metaphor in the poem and all that comes after it is employed to show the poet's discovery: "by analogy an identity between objects which is partial, though it should be considerable, and proceeds to an identification which is complete."

"Burns' poem," he continued, "is mostly similes":

> O my love is like a red, red rose
>   That's newly sprung in June;
> O my love is like the melodie
>   That's sweetly played in tune.

"The purpose of the simile, with its use of *like* and *as,* is "scrupulously to keep the identification partial."

"The trouble with a well-known poem by Longfellow," he continued, "is different but obvious." He read:

> Life is real! Life is earnest!
>   And the grave is not its goal;
> Dust they are to dust returneth,
>   Was not spoken of the soul.

Do Not Go Beyond this Point

There is nothing here that cannot and has not been expressed in prose; whereas "poetry is the means by which we express that which we cannot in prose."

One morning, Ransom came in, greeted the class, and made the following statement:

> As I came down West End Avenue from the grocery store yesterday afternoon, I saw a sign which warned: "Do not go beyond this point unless you know the way is clear." Like most prose, this was almost perfect pentameter, so I began to think I could make a few changes and compose a poem. After working and worrying with it for a while, making a few changes, I came up with the following version.

And he wrote on the board:

O: do not gó	A
Beyónd this píer	B
Untíl you knów	A
The wáy is cléar.	B

"What have I done? With a few changes I have made perfect iambic dimeter [a line with two poetic feet composed of two unstressed and two stressed syllables] and an ABAB rhyme scheme" [the first and third and the second and fourth lines rhyme].

"You have made a poem," replied a student.

"No, I haven't. I've given rhyme and meter to prose. Just as in Longfellow's 'Psalm of Life,' there's nothing here that can't be expressed in prose."

Ransom continued in this manner for the remainder of the semester—pointing out the structure and the texture and explaining the specific qualities of verse that make for good or bad poetry.

The next two years were busy, happy ones. The Office of Admissions had an efficient staff, and we tried to organize the process of recruiting and admitting students exactly as Purdy and Fields wanted. After I became familiar with the academic budgets of the undergraduate colleges, Purdy left that job almost entirely to me.

In October 1963, I was attending the meeting of the South Atlantic Modern Language Association when George Harper, chairman of the English Department at the University of North Carolina, at Chapel Hill, asked me to teach in summer school the next year. Hugh Holman, who taught Southern and Modern American literature, the areas of my specialization, was to be academic vice-chancellor of the university and George needed someone to teach his classes. Things were fairly quiet at Vanderbilt, and Purdy gave me permission to go to Chapel Hill. I, my mother, Arlease, and our three boys struck out for North Carolina, spending the first night in Asheville and arriving in Chapel Hill at midafternoon the next day. I found the house we had rented, and we unloaded the car. Half way up the lawn I saw a rolled-up newspaper. After getting a Coke out of the cooler we had brought with us and settling in a comfortable chair, I opened the paper. I almost fainted because there in big black letters was a headline which read: "Dr. Dan Young Receives One and One-Half Million Dollar Grant." At first I did not believe what I had read; then I thought some of my friends had played a trick on me and had a fake headline printed in the paper. Finally I read the accompanying story and found there was a Dr. Dan Young in the medical school, and it was he who had received the grant.

Only a few times in my life have I been happier than I was that summer. First of all, I was doing full-time teaching for the first time in my career. Second—and best of all—I had bright, experienced, well-prepared students. Third, I had been assigned to teach only classes in my area of concentration—a seminar in the Southern Renaissance and a senior-graduate lecture course in the modern American novel. No committees; no administration.

One Friday night about halfway through the term, I got a call from the other Dr. Dan Young saying he had just received a call from Nashville that was intended for me. He had taken a Nashville number that I was to call immediately. I called the number and found I was talking to Professor E. H. Duncan. Duncan had become acting chairman of the department after Randall Stewart's death the day before. "I must have a full-time teacher of American and Southern literature," Duncan said. "If you'll take the position, you may have it. Otherwise, I must get busy and find someone else." Despite my sorrow over Randall's death, it wasn't unexpected, since he had been ill for more than a year. It took me only a moment to accept Duncan's offer. I didn't even ask what the salary would be.

After I returned to Nashville, I talked to Ed and found that he had scheduled me to teach a section of sophomore-level American literature, a section of Southern literature, and a graduate seminar. The teaching schedule and class times were excellent. The salary was, as I had expected, less than I had made in administration. But I was happy. Arlease and I were agreed that if I ever was to have a teaching career—and I had always wanted one—I should have it now.

In addition, M. Thomas Inge and I had discussed doing the Twayne book on Davidson, and I had already begun looking through the Davidson papers while Inge got together a bibliography of work by and about Davidson. Inge's work neared completion. Meanwhile, I had found some interesting material in the papers. I discovered that Davidson had written five complete drafts of "Lee in the Mountains" before publishing the book. I got busy using the drafts to trace the development of the poem from a fifty-line statement of its structure to a sophisticated, suggestive, connotative poem of 121 lines. I was preparing an essay for a scholarly journal when Ed Duncan suggested that I combine my essay and Tom's bibliography in a small book and submit it to Vanderbilt University Press for publication in time to give it to Davidson when he retired the next spring. Tom and I agreed, and at the next faculty meeting, Ed announced our plans. A few days later, Davidson saw me in the post office and asked about the progress of my essay. I told him I'd completed a draft and given it to a typist. He wanted to know what I was calling the essay, and I replied, "The Evolution of 'Lee in the Mountains.'"

"My God," he exploded; "you know I don't like that word. *Evolution*—no one but Darwin or some other scientist would use that word."

"But what would you have me call it?"

He pondered a minute, then said: "The Making of 'Lee in the Mountains.'"

I couldn't help thinking of what college students would do with *making* and *making out*. "Professor Davidson," I said, "Can you see the title page 'The Making of "Lee in the Mountains"' by Thomas Daniel Young?"

"Why, that's all right," he replied without a trace of a grin; "Tom Inge's name is going to be on the title page, too, isn't it?" He had missed my point, so I said good day and left.

Despite Ransom's telling me when I approached him in the spring of 1961 for permission to write his authorized biography, "Oh, that's fine, but I don't think there's enough there," I had continued to gather material about him. In the early spring of 1968, realizing that I had enough essays about Ransom and his contribution to American letters by such authors as Warren, Brooks, Jarrell, Matthiessen, Rubin, Lanning, and others to publish a book, I requested permission to use the complete bibliography of Ransom (done as a thesis by Mildred Brooks Peters under my direction) and submitted the essays and bibliography to Louisiana State University Press.

Another way to gather material for the biography was to talk to everyone who had had Ransom as a teacher. I soon found a broad division of opinion. Those of a literary persuasion considered Ransom their most gifted teacher, while many with lesser literary interests found him uninteresting, eccentric, effeminate. In an attempt to get a broader perspective, I decided to volunteer to speak to Vanderbilt alumni clubs whenever I was asked. To my surprise, there was broad interest in my suggested topic: "Vanderbilt's Literary Tradition: The Fugitives, the Agrarians, and the New Critics." Before I realized how broadly and deeply involved in this project I had become, I had accepted invitations to speak in such places as New York, Washington, New Orleans, and Los Angeles. I would summarize these literary movements that had originated at Vanderbilt and explain that they were the most important that had occurred in America in the twentieth century. I always added that Ransom was perhaps the mastermind behind them. Again, I found the division I had discovered nearer home—those with particular literary interests respected Ransom, and those with little or no interest in writing or literature were at best neutral on the subject. Another trend I noted was that most of Ransom's students were reluctant to talk about him; they preferred to talk about Edwin Mims, chairman of the English Department and a popular teacher of literature for more than a quarter of a century.

One night, in Conway, Arkansas, I asked a middle-aged woman if she had had one of Ransom's classes. "No, I didn't," she said. Before I could say anything else, she said she'd had Professor Mims, then told me the following tale.

> One day, Professor Mims was pontificating about "Crossing the Bar," when suddenly he stopped and looked at me, sitting in the front row.
> "Young lady," he said; "why aren't you taking notes?"
> "I don't have to," I replied. "My mother gave me hers."

In the spring of 1968, a meeting of former Agrarians was held at the University of Dallas. I was one of the scholars assigned to determine whether these writers still held the views they had expressed in the two Agrarian symposia, *I'll Take My Stand* (1930) and *Who Owns America?* (1936). Tate, Warren, Lytle, and Ransom attended. Mrs. Frank Owsley was there, representing her deceased husband. Lyle Lanier could not be located. Donald Davidson, in a Nashville hospital, gave me a ten-page paper assuring the group that adherence to the views of the Agrarians was the only means of ensuring the continuance of modern civilization.

One morning, as Tate, Ransom, and I were eating breakfast at our motel, Tate looked at me and then at Ransom. "John," he said, "you had better appoint an authorized biographer. At least you can help him keep the record straight." When Ransom left to attend the meeting, I followed him, assuring him of my continuing interest in writing his biography. "I'm game if you are," he said with a twinkle in his eye. Thus, I became involved in a project that would occupy me for the next ten years.

John Crowe Ransom: Critical Essays and a Bibliography was published in 1968 by Louisiana State University Press. At about the same time, I discovered the Ransom family papers in the Tennessee State Library. This collection contains every letter Ransom wrote home from the time he enrolled in Vanderbilt until the early 1960s (several hundred were written from Oxford while Ransom was a Rhodes scholar). This was a valuable find, and I received Ransom's permission to have it copied. Reading the letters carefully took all of my spare time during the next two years. Of course, I reread the Ransom essays and poems and the most important critical studies of his work.

In the fall of 1971, I took a semester's leave and traveled to the colleges and universities with Ransom material—Harvard, Yale, Princeton, Indiana, Kenyon, Texas, and Stanford. At each institution I looked through the material, selected what I thought would be helpful, and had copies sent to me at Vanderbilt. When I returned in 1972, I had enough material to keep me busy until I completed my second three-year term as chairman, on July 1, 1972. Although being chairman was a time-consuming position, most of the duties I performed in that capacity were interesting. My least pleasant duty was serving as chairman of the departmental tenure committee. The requirements were strenuous; during my two terms, only four persons received tenure. Not only must the candidate for tenure have earned his Ph.D. degree and have published at least one book, his work must have been well received by the reviewers in scholarly journals. Every time I went through this procedure, I was reminded of the manner in which I had been given tenure.

Shortly after finishing my second term as chairman, I was appointed Gertrude Conaway Vanderbilt Professor of English. Just when I was rejoicing over all the free time I expected to have to work on my book, Dean Fields asked me to serve as the first director of the Vanderbilt-in-England Program. Although I wanted to spend another year in England, I hesitated, thinking the position would be too time-consuming. I was pleasantly surprised to learn that we would not go over in a group, which meant that Arlease, Kyle (a student in the program), and I had a three-week vacation in London before going on to Leeds. I arrived in the pleasant, roomy house we'd rented in time to get the students placed in British residence halls. When the students came, they registered for classes in the departments in which they were majoring at Vanderbilt. Since I was to teach in the department of American literature, I went to the head professor of American literature and found that I had been assigned twenty third-year students (all of whom would take examinations in the spring) and that I was to give twelve public lectures on American writers of my choice. I chose Hawthorne, Melville, Whitman, Dickinson, Twain, James, Dreiser, Crane, Hemingway, Fitzgerald, Faulkner, and Eliot. I was told that in Britain James and Eliot are considered English writers; so I substituted Ezra Pound and Wallace Stevens.

After meeting the students I was to tutor (my job was to assist them in preparing for the examination next spring), I decided that I could do best what I was expected to do by having small discussion groups of five students each one hour a week. (It didn't escape my attention that such a schedule would save me fifteen hours a week.) Therefore, I assigned the books we were to discuss and strongly suggested that they attend my lectures. Since I had taught the books I was lecturing on many times, the lectures required only minimum preparation. Also, the books we would be discussing were standard

American classics. A few minutes' review was all the preparation it would take.

Our American students lived in residence halls, where each was assigned a British tutor. This meant I had little responsibility for the students except check on them occasionally and, on special occasions, have Arlease prepare dinners and parties to entertain them. My duties to the University, then, were fairly well confined for the first six months from ten to twelve on Tuesday and Thursday and one night of lecture about every second week. Unlike American students, British students spend about half of their time on vacation, reading the books tutors have assigned. Rather than having to devote more time to my school work, as I had expected, I spent far less.

I took an upstairs bedroom as a study, spread my materials everywhere, and devoted five full days and two afternoons to reviewing, rereading, and writing a rough draft of the book I'd been working on for eight or nine years. When we arrived back in Nashville the following July, I was ready to take a semester's leave. My dean had assured me that I could take the winter semester off at full salary, and I had received a Fulbright grant to pay my expenses. I was thus prepared to spend an entire semester in Gambier, interviewing Mr. Ransom and checking on the facts I had garnered from his letters and essays. Most of all, I wanted to get his reaction to my reading of his poems.

CHAPTER

12

Reading Good Books

On January 2, 1975, I began driving to Gambier, Ohio, expecting to arrive there sometime late that evening. As I neared Columbus, however, it began to snow, and by the time I had driven through the city, driving was so treacherous that I stopped for the night. I asked the desk clerk how far I was from Gambier and what was the best route to get there. He told me it was thirty or forty miles, but that, because of road conditions, the best way might not be the shortest. I asked him if he thought the roads would be cleared by tomorrow. He thought I-71 would but didn't know about state route 220. I bid him good night and went to my room. After a full day of driving, I was exhausted and fell asleep immediately.

I didn't awaken until about eight o'clock, and it was nearly ten before I got on the road. The interstate, I was glad to see, had been cleared. Except for the piles of snow by the side of the road, one would not have known it had snowed. When I got to 220, I saw that it too had been cleared. I arrived before noon and checked into the room at the Alumni House that my son, Kyle, had reserved for me.

Over the next few weeks, I learned how beautiful it is to watch snow-covered terrain and walk over it—when you don't have to drive through it to work or don't have to worry about the car not starting or the roof of the house leaking. During the next four months, I did not start my car a half-dozen times. I had no need to; the cafe in which I ate was a few steps from the Alumni House, as was the post office, and John Crowe Ransom lived about a hundred yards away.

As soon as I reached Gambier, I went to call on Ransom. I met his wife, Robb, and their daughter, Helen. After a few minutes of conversation, he and I retired to his study, and he immediately set down some ground rules for the interviews: (1) he was not going to speak into a tape recorder because "one of those gadgets tongue-ties me"; (2) he would discuss the contents of his critical essays and books but would not attempt to analyze any of his poems; (3) he would talk to me about his literary career—how and why he wrote a particular poem, essay, or book, any details related to the *Kenyon Review,* but "I don't believe anyone would be interested in the minutae of my personal life." This last restriction bothered me somewhat, though Robert Penn Warren had already warned me that I was undertaking a very difficult project. "You can't write a good biography of a good man," he said, "and don't start looking for a skeleton in John's closet, because there isn't any closet."

Almost immediately, we established a routine: I would talk with him in the afternoon and write notes (in longhand) on what he had said. After dinner, I would attempt to put in some order the notes I had taken that afternoon. Early the next morning, I would attempt to add specific details and direct quotations to the rough draft I had written the previous day.

I soon found that there were some subjects Ransom would speak on in great detail: his family, his early life, his days at Vanderbilt and Oxford, his teaching experiences. He even gave details and anecdotes related to the founding, development, and editing of the *Kenyon Review.* He also responded freely and helpfully about his essays and reading. On one subject, however, he remained silent. When I showed him an analysis of one of his poems, his answer was always something like: "Well, now, I'm surprised you could find all that in that poem." The greatest compliment he ever paid me was after he had read a monograph I had written about his poetry. "Now, that's very good because you mostly let me talk for myself." What he was really saying was that I had quoted a great deal of his poetry and had added little comment of my own.

I was perplexed by Ransom's reluctance to talk about his poetry. To some extent I still am. Thinking back on an event that occurred one afternoon when we were talking in his study, I think I now understand his reasons for not discussing his poetry. We were deeply involved in some questions that particularly interested him when the telephone rang. He answered it, listened for about a minute, then said, "Will you hold on just a second?" As he walked to the bookcases across the room, he said to me: "Some young lady teacher from the college in Murfreesboro wants to know what 'Bells for John Whiteside's Daughter' means." He walked to the bookcase, pulled out a copy of his *Selected Poems,* and went back to his chair. "Are you still there?" he asked, picking up the phone again. Then he read every word of the poem to her (she was paying for the long-distance call); then he said, "That's as close as I could come to its meaning," he said when he'd finished, then hung up.

At first, I was shocked by this incident; but after I got back to my room and had thought about how he had read the poem, I understood it better than I ever had. The first thing I thought of was Warren's statement that "Bells" is really about "The emotional distance between *astonishment* and *vexation* and why the narrator has travelled from one to the other."

Ransom read the first stanza:

> There was such speed in her little body,
> And such lightness in her footfall,
> It is no wonder her brown study
> Astonishes us all.

When he got to the word "astonishes," he added emphasis to indicate the state of feeling of the uninvolved bystander, the point of view of the poem, who is unrelated to the little girl but who definitely changed by her death. He and the other members of the community who are not related to her remember her vitality and energy and are surprised (Ransom is right, of course; "astonishes" more closely describes their exact feelings) to see her so still. Her "brown study" restates the contrast. She is brown because she has been browned by the sun; she has a suntan, which we associate with health, life, and energy. At first, the narrator thinks only of her lost energy; but after a moment of reflection, in which he recounts the activities in which she has been involved (his attitude makes him give some symbolic overtones to her commonplace activities), he and the community adopt an entirely different attitude toward her:

> But now go the bells and we are ready,
> In one house we are sternly stopped
> To say we are vexed at her brown study,
> Lying so primly propped.

When Ransom comes in his reading to "vexed," his voice reveals the narrator's and the community's change of attitude. Now they are angry, confused, irritated, and all the other meanings carried by "vexed." After looking at the small, dead girl for a minute or two, they realize that her change is more than a brief rest; it is permanent. Thus, their attitude changes, and the nature of that change is best conveyed by "vexed." First, they are merely astonished that she now acts differently. Now they realize why she does so: she is dead, her rest is permanent. They are deeply disturbed ("vexed"). They wonder why death, which is usually reserved for the elderly, had to happen to her. Why was she not allowed to live? How can one reconcile such actions with an omnipotent, all-loving God?

When I wrote such explanations as this, Ransom always demurred: "I am surprised you can see all of that in there." I am convinced, however, that something like what I have written is what he was trying to suggest to the young lady on the telephone and why he always insisted: "If I could express what I am trying to express in this poem in prose, I would have written prose." Ransom's basic critical principle was: Any genuine work of art merits any reading a perceptive reader can read *into* it with logic and feeling.

As my semester with Mr. Ransom drew to an end, I began going through my manuscript again, trying to get it as nearly right as I could this time. To announce that a biography of Ransom was in the works, I began publishing what I considered the best of the chapters in what is known in the trade as "quality" journals. By the time I thought the manuscript was ready for a publisher to see, I had published portions of it in the *Southern Review, Sewanee Review, Georgia Review, Spectrum,* and *Mississippi Review.*

In the fall of 1975—nearly fifteen years after I had thought of writing the biography and had begun tentatively to collect the material, and ten years after I had begun devoting to it all the time I could spare or steal from my teaching—I turned in to my editor at Louisiana State University Press a typescript of about 850 pages. The book appeared in late 1976, to good critical reviews. George Core, editor of the *Sewanee Review,* wrote: "A fine piece of work which will be the standard biography of Ransom for years to come—at least for this century. . . . Professor Young has done an extraordinarily thorough job of scholarship in establishing the essential facts of Ransom's life." Louis D. Rubin, Jr., of the University of North Carolina at Chapel Hill, added: "It is a distinguished piece of work. . . . What Young has done [is] execute a thorough job of research on Ransom's life and career, and join this with a quite lucid explanation of Ransom's major theories and writings about literature."

The book's greatest achievement, perhaps, was winning the Jules

Landry Award for 1976, for "The most significant contribution to the study of Southern letters" that year.

After this project was completed, I could devote my attention and most of my efforts to teaching. I had a seminar on some topic or figure of twentieth-century American literature on Monday afternoons, and taught an advanced undergraduate course—usually the modern American novel, modern American poetry, or the Southern renaissance—on Mondays, Wednesdays, and Fridays. I conferred with students in my office on those same days. Although the undergraduate class grew to be quite large—from one to three hundred—the chairman furnished assistants to check the attendance and grade the papers; so I usually had every afternoon, as well as Tuesdays, Thursdays, and Saturdays, free for my research and writing. As Gertrude Conaway Vanderbilt Professor, I could usually get a semester off when I wanted it. I took one semester off to lecture at twelve British universities and another to lecture at universities in Scandinavia, France, and West Germany. I remember my embarrassment when I discovered that my introductory lectures on Fitzgerald, Hemingway, Faulkner, Ransom, and other modern American writers were too elementary for my audiences. Most of the students to whom I talked were majoring in American literature or American studies and had two or three years in American literature and wanted to hear papers on such topics as "Faulkner and the Community," "The Affirmative Ending of Hemingway's *The Sun Also Rises*," or Ransom's "Theories of the Nature and Uses of Poetry." I had to rewrite the introductory lectures I had prepared before leaving the United States after arriving in Europe. I well remember the endless days and nights I spent researching and preparing those lectures. What began as a lark almost ended in a nightmare. I ended the visit to England with three advanced lectures before the American Studies Association of Western Europe, at the University of Liverpool: "Ransom's Poetry and the Modern

Sensibility," "The Significance of Quentin Compson in *The Sound and the Fury*," and "Errors of Point of View in Fitzgerald's *The Great Gatsby*." With this happy ending, I think the lecture trip was, on the whole, successful, and parts of it were even pleasing and enjoyable.

In my undergraduate course in the Southern Renaissance, I emphasized William Faulkner, Eudora Welty, Flannery O'Connor, Katherine Anne Porter, Walker Percy and the writers who had connections with Vanderbilt and the important literary movements that originated there: John Crowe Ransom, Allen Tate, Robert Penn Warren, and Andrew Lytle. I also devoted considerable time to a younger group which had been influenced by the older men: Jesse Stuart, Randall Jarrell, Peter Taylor, and Madison Jones. The course became known as the "Vanderbilt course" and attracted students from the disciplines of religion, philosophy, law, science, medicine, and others, and, as a result, became a very large class. Because of its size—and despite the fact that I was furnished sufficient assistance so that my primary function was lecturing—there were some disadvantages to a large lecture section. It troubled me that I never got to know many of the students. On one occasion, I recall, a young lady I thought I'd never seen before came by the office and asked if I would write her a recommendation to graduate school. I asked her if she'd ever had a class with me. "Yes," she responded. "I had your Southern lit last semester." When I asked how she had done in the course, she said, "I made an A." I was appalled. These were the first words I had spoken to her, and she not only was an English major, but when she left I had my assistant check her records; she had A's in almost *all* of her courses.

The situation was vastly different in my smaller, advanced undergraduate classes, in which most of the students were English majors, and in the graduate classes. Not only were we well acquainted, but I advised them on all kinds of problems, both professional and personal.

Soon after becoming chairman at Southern Mississippi, I was teaching a section of the second half of the American literature survey; and the first paper I assigned was on *The Adventures of Huckleberry Finn*. The students were asked not to use any outside sources; rather, they were to read the book closely, then try to determine (and inform me) why it was considered an American classic. As I read the papers, I came upon one that dumbfounded me. It was the best paper by an undergraduate I had ever read. The student discussed, concisely, plausibly, and convincingly, the importance of the river (and the contrast between it and the villages on the banks of the Mississippi), the humor, the development of the major characters and the weaknesses of the ending. He argued that the first two-thirds of the book was good enough to make the book a classic despite its "ineffectual, ambiguous ending." When I returned the papers the next day, I called the student's name and asked him to come by the office. I was surprised when I learned the name of the student; I had hardly heard from him in class. When he came in, I asked him what his major was, and he said he hadn't decided. I invited him to major in English. "I guess I should," he replied. "I *do* like to read." I told him to go to the registrar's office, declare his major, and come back to my office. He did, and from that moment on, I planned his schedule, having him take the courses to give him a major in English, a minor in French, and two years of German. When he graduated, his other teachers and I recommended him highly to the University of Mississippi, where he studied for his M.A., and to Emory, where he received his Ph.D. Since graduation, he has had a distinguished career in teaching, writing, and administration.

This experience could be multiplied at least a dozen times. Once I had a young lady who was as close to being a genius as anyone I've ever met. She had entered college at fifteen and was taking an extra course each quarter in order to graduate in three years. Almost any book one mentioned that had been published in the past five years, she had read, and she answered any question one asked in class without effort. She graduated in three years and with the help of the English faculty at Southern, received a graduate fellowship to Tulane University. Soon after I went to Delta State, a friend of mine at Tulane telephoned to say that the student had completed requirements for the Ph.D., but the dean of the graduate school was hesitant to award the degree because she was only twenty-one. He asked me if we would give her a three-year nontenure-track appointment in the English Department. After consulting the chairman of the Department, I told the dean that, beginning the following fall, we would. She came and stayed the three years, went back and received her degree, and taught at an outstanding Midwestern university until she married and moved back to the South, where she is one of the most respected scholars in her field.

I will mention only two other examples from among the students who were at Southern Mississippi during my tenure there. One was a young man from New York whom I taught at Keesler Air Force Base. After completing his enlistment in the Air Force, he came to Southern not knowing what he should major in. I convinced him to concentrate in English. He completed the requirements for the bachelor's and master's degrees with us, and upon strong recommendations from the English Department faculty of the University of Southern Mississippi, was awarded a fellowship at Northwestern University. After receiving his Ph.D., he returned to Delta State University, where I had a young lady as a student whom I persuaded to major in English rather than elementary education. They married and their family and ours have been close friends ever since.

Another student had earned his bachelor's at Southern between the time I was a student there and when I returned, and then a master's in education from Alabama. He returned to do a master's in

English because he wasn't content to continue high-school teaching. I had known him slightly when I was a student at Southern (his father was principal of the demonstration school) but was unaware of his ability. Because his grades in English were above a B average, his recommendations were excellent, and his GED scores were impressive, the admissions committee accepted him. During the second quarter, he took my seminar in the modern American novel and wrote an excellent essay on *The Sun Also Rises*. When I returned his paper with adulatory comments, he came by and asked if he could write his thesis on Hemingway. I encouraged him to do so, and we talked several times about the approach to Hemingway he might take in his paper. He thought he should write on "the author as character." He continued to do good work in his seminars, and the following spring he turned in a 150-page paper that developed the same thesis that Phillip Young develops in his *Ernest Hemingway*. Had my student's work not appeared several months before Young's, I'm sure he would have been accused of plagiarism. He was tired of going to school, he said; and besides, he had to earn some money to support his growing family. Therefore, we gave him an instructorship in the department. An excellent teacher, he always received the highest evaluations from his students. When my family and I were moving to Delta State, my first official act was to offer Professor Hitt the chairmanship of the English Department. He recommended that he be allowed to bring this student (Harvey Craft) as an instructor, and I enthusiastically agreed. From the time he began to teach at Southern, through his tenure at Delta State, Harvey's family and mine were the best of friends. Even after he had completed his Ph.D., and while he was holding important positions at several respected universities, we continued to meet each other as often as we could.

As I have mentioned, one of my undergraduate classes was so large that I did not get to know the students very well; but there *were* a few who came by the office to get acquainted, a practice that enabled me to get reactions from the class. Their opinions were helpful to me because I could gauge to what extent I was getting across the material to a large group. I also taught a graduate seminar and an advanced undergraduate course. Since I varied the subject matter in these courses as much as possible, I had a number of the same students three or four times, and I got to know them well. I required that they come by the office two or three times each term to discuss their papers and reports. Many also visited in our home and attended the parties we gave for visiting writers and for students completing the requirements for the Ph.D. Many of these students have visited me when they came back to Vanderbilt and have written while they were away. As a consequence, I count among my friends outstanding lawyers, doctors, physicists, chemists, and business executives across the country. Recently, after I had made a speech in Houston, Texas, for the Alumni Association, fifteen of my former students—and there were only three professors among them—took me out for drinks and dinner.

Many of my graduate seminars were concerned with such Southern writers as Welty and Faulkner and the best-known of the Vanderbilt writers, such as Ransom, Tate, Warren, Davidson, Peter Taylor, and Randall Jarrell. The world's best collection by and about last group is in the Special Collections of Vanderbilt Library and the Tennessee State Archives in Nashville. I directed almost fifty dissertations, about half of which have been published, in whole or in part.

Although a statement by a former student at the roast that accompanied my retirement ("Professor Young carefully placed his students in colleges and universities so that he could travel from Washington to Houston, Texas, and never be more than a meal's distance from one of them") is somewhat inaccurate, I did what I could to assist them in finding positions and helping them get promotions and tenure. I not only wrote recommendations for them, I also read, when asked, the essays and manuscripts that they prepared for publication and suggested journals to which materials should be sent. In addition, I have co-edited five books with my former students. Finally, I am convinced that my closest and most enduring friendships are those I share with my former students.

At the time of my retirement from Vanderbilt after twenty-five years of service, I suggested my career had been both my vocation and my avocation. I had earned my living by doing what I enjoy best: reading good books, then talking and writing about them. The reporter who interviewed me called his article "T. D. Young, the Good Reader." But no one realized better than I that I had not learned to read, even as well as I had, without effort. I was flattered that he thought I was a good reader. Often, after I had talked many times about a modern novel to my classes, and even after I had tried to express my attitudes in writing, as I did in *The Past and the Present* (1981), I realized how far inferior my reading was to the authors' intentions.

I realize, too, that whatever reading skill I have was not easily or quickly acquired. Even in high school, when my English teacher required that I read British and American classics, both novels and poetry, I enjoyed them; but I did not truly differentiate between their quality and that of the Zane Grey novels I was reading.

I first became acutely aware of the genuine merits of a good book during the time I was involved in the reading exercises with my Air Force friends at Land's End. The skills I acquired there were greatly enhanced by my experience with J. Dover Wilson. It was at that point that these skills became definitely and permanently a part of me. I continued to practice what I had learned while observing Donald Davidson's approach to literature. No doubt, I am one of the thousands of readers who were permanently affected by the New Criticism. In my teaching, as well as in my reading and writing, I have attempted to follow the theories advocated by John Crowe Ransom in his *The World's Body* and practiced by Donald Davidson in the classroom.

Not only has reading been my most satisfying pleasure, it has been, in the words of John Crowe Ransom, a means of cognition. It has helped me to know the world. Literature has taught me not to rely entirely on science or social science for my understanding and appreciation of the society in which I grew up. The sociological term, "plane of living," which places Mississippi at the bottom of the social and economic scale, reveals only a part of the truth, just as science teaches us only about our animal life. Science does not reveal that we are "whole and indefeasible objects," as literature does. Social science describes the economic values that are important to our lives, but only the fine arts allow us to know the aesthetic values that differentiate us from other animals.

Measured by the economic values, the plane of living, the little Mississippi village in which I grew up would be very near the bottom of the scale. But the quality of life in my hometown was very high indeed, a fact I have come fully to realize only late in life. As a youth I came to feel a genuine affection for my family, which included not only the members of my immediate household, but also the entire family connection, including twelve aunts and uncles and dozens of cousins. I realize now that I was then a particularized someone who belonged to a specific place and that I participated fully in the affairs of that community—its schools, churches, social and political organizations, and that all of the people who lived there were my friends and neighbors. It was there that I came to know love.

Not long ago I returned to the community in which I grew up to attend a funeral. Although I had spent little time there for the past fifty years, almost everyone I met asked me, "Aren't you Dan, Dr. Young's son?" As I looked at one who made the inquiry, and using the same basis for reaching a conclusion he had, family resemblance, I answered, "Yes, and aren't you the son or grandson of Peggy Fulton?" "I am," he responded, "her son Nolan and as youngsters we used to play together when I visited your neighbors, the Garriguses, my mother's family." I soon learned that he was a retired surgeon from the United States Army Medical Corps, and he, that I was an emeritus professor from Vanderbilt. "Isn't it strange," he said, "that you followed my family's profession and I, yours?" Then I realized, as I had many times before, that I knew the people of that community better than those of any city I had lived in since. This realization focused my thoughts and reminescences into the channel that resulted in this book and persuaded me that I was indeed very fortunate to have grown up "in the state the nation can best afford to do without."

www.ingramcontent.com/pod-product-compliance
Lightning Source LLC
Chambersburg PA
CBHW030345240426
43661CB00052B/1748